"In a world crying out for kindness and belonging, this is a book needed for our times. *Sweet Like Jasmine* is a gift, a beautiful remembrance that God treasures each of our broken hearts in His sweeping story of redemption."

Ann Voskamp,
New York Times bestselling author of
The Broken Way and *One Thousand Gifts*

"*Sweet Like Jasmine* feels like having a cup of tea with a kind and brave friend who reminds you of God's love, His grace, and how His unseen hand is in all of our stories. It's beautiful and powerful, life giving and heart freeing, deeply personal and soul-touching relatable. I read it one weekend, savoring every word, and I didn't want it to end."

Holley Gerth,
Wall Street Journal bestselling author of
The Powerful Purpose of Introverts

"Bonnie has a gift! Her stories draw you in from the start, and her raw honesty captures the heart of all who are looking for love and belonging in a culture of loneliness and isolation. This book is a healing balm of beauty from brokenness."

Rebekah Lyons,
bestselling author of *Rhythms of Renewal* and *You Are Free*

"If you've struggled with feeling as if you don't fit in or aren't good enough, Bonnie's story of finding beauty and belonging in her brokenness will encourage your heart. I loved her poignant retelling of both the sweet and the bitter memories from her childhood, and how she can look back and see God's goodness and faithfulness in the midst of it."

Crystal Paine,
New York Times bestselling author, podcaster, and
founder of MoneySavingMom.com

"Bonnie Gray is an engaging storyteller who reminds us of the grace woven through each chapter of our lives. This book is both poetic and insightful. Beautiful and honest. A worthy companion through the wilderness of learning to find our identity. Through stories, letters, cultural insights, and reflections, *Sweet Like Jasmine* generously provides much-needed language and permission to embrace the wholeness of who we are."

Morgan Harper Nichols,
uthor of *All Along You Were Blooming*

"No one tells a story like Bonnie Gray! Join her on a journey of vulnerability, discovery, and a growing awareness of God's redemptive power in our lives. Along the way, you'll see that it's right in our broken places that God shows himself strong."

Kathi Lipp,
bestselling author and speaker

"This is one of those books that will stay with you long after you've turned the final page. Bonnie's story is achingly beautiful—not only because it's true, but because it is truly transformative. Our two life stories couldn't be more different, yet Bonnie's story is also mine. And it's yours. This is a story of the secrets and shame we all carry, and how God is working—always working—to bring beauty out of every broken moment. This book is a treasure."

Jennifer Dukes Lee,
author of *Growing Slow* and *It's All Under Control*

"*Sweet Like Jasmine* is a love story that will bring beauty and healing to tender places in the heart and deeper compassion for those who have ever felt unlovable or unworthy."

Melissa Michaels,
New York Times bestselling author of
Love the Home You Have and *Dwelling*

"A beautiful book with thought-provoking reflections, *Sweet Like Jasmine* is a captivating blend of powerful story and hope-filled self-discovery. I couldn't put it down!"

Renee Swope,
bestselling author of *A Confident Heart*

"Bonnie has often led the way to freedom and truth by going there first herself. Her ability to invite us as readers into her stories, and therefore into our own stories, makes this world a better, more healed place."

Annie F. Downs,
New York Times bestselling author of *That Sounds Fun*

Sweet Like Jasmine

Bonnie Gray

HARVEST HOUSE PUBLISHERS
EUGENE, OREGON

Cover design by Faceout Studio

Cover photo © Sveta_Aho / Gettyimages

Interior design by KUHN Design Group

The author is represented by Alive Literary Agency, www.aliveliterary.com

Names and minor details have been changed in the real-life stories shared in this book to protect the privacy of the individuals mentioned.

For bulk, special sales, or ministry purchases, please call 1-800-547-8979. Email: Customerservice@hhpbooks.com.

Sweet Like Jasmine
Copyright © 2021 by Bonnie Lee Gray
Published by Harvest House Publishers
Eugene, Oregon 97408
www.harvesthousepublishers.com

ISBN 978-0-7369-8342-6 (pbk.)
ISBN 978-0-7369-8343-3 (eBook)
ISBN 978-0-7369-8587-1 (eAudio)

Library of Congress Control Number: 2021935220

To Jesus
my Loving Savior
who understood my loneliness
and tenderly calls me His beloved

To Eric
my beloved soulmate
because writing a new story
with you makes life beautiful

To Josh and Caleb
my beloved sons
because being your mom is a joy, seeing
God's light shining within you

And to my kindred readers
because we are all simply walking each other home

Contents

Introduction

I've never truly felt beautiful or beloved. That sounds like something only people with perfect families in nice-looking houses get to experience. I wanted to grow up and leave behind everything that made me feel weird, flawed, and broken. So, I did all the things I was supposed to do and built a life that looked like everyone else's.

I did this so I could have a chance at being normal. So I could belong. So I could be loved. But something unexpected happened. As I tried to build the life I thought I should have, I discovered that I was not whole—not even close.

Even though I was grateful for everything in my life, I didn't feel happy. I didn't feel like I belonged anywhere. Instead of joy, I felt lonely and uninspired.

Somewhere along the way, I lost the things that make life beautiful and meaningful, that make us come alive with beauty and joy.

Once I had my second baby and became a mom to two boys, I figured it was too late for me. I was a parent now. We can't all choose our childhoods, but it was time to make the next generation better. *Just get over yourself, Bonnie,* I told myself. And that is how I gave up on myself.

But God didn't give up on me. This is a story of how He tenderly gathered all the bruised and broken fragments I had tried to throw away. This is the story of God whispering, *What no one wants, I cherish. I love every part of you. You are worth loving. You are My beloved.*

As we take this journey together, I pray that you will hear this loving whisper come alive in you too, as you open your heart to your own story and embrace all you are created to be.

CELEBRATE THE JOURNEY

Join me. Listen to your life and celebrate everything that has happened to you, because it is through those events that God speaks. Together, we will go on an intimate journey to recognize your belovedness, realizing that flaws are not meant to be erased, but worth loving and even celebrating. The things that make us different and broken are the very parts that make us beautiful and bind us together.

This soulful journey is a powerful self-discovery experience made more meaningful by sharing it with friends, as you pause in the busyness of life and discover the gift of your stories. I encourage you to read this book with a gathering of kindred spirits to connect deeply using "Reflect and Share" questions I have tucked in each chapter to help spark conversation. Why? Because when we share our stories, we create a place of refuge in the world that says, "I see you. Rest awhile. You are at home with me."

It's never too late to be you.

It's never too late to begin again.

It's never too late to be loved.

By the time you finish walking through this journey, you will gather a collection of your own stories to celebrate God's story in you—marveling at the glimmering mosaic of His love in your life, bringing beauty into the world.

For me, this journey began in a way I never could have predicted. Unexpectedly.

Chapter 1

Birth Certificate

My mother, *Ah-Ma*, was a mail-order bride from Hong Kong, and my father, *Bah-Ba*, worked as a busboy in a noodle shop in San Francisco Chinatown. I rarely tell people about any of this; it only leads to more questions: *How did your mother meet your dad? Why did your dad leave? Where is he now?* I never wanted to answer these questions because I didn't know the answers. No one ever told me. And what little I did know, I wouldn't want to tell anybody.

If you had asked me what my father looked like, I wouldn't even be able to really tell you for sure. It was a long time since I last saw him.

I didn't have a single photograph of my father by the time it was all over. My mother was cutting up every picture we had of him as I sat on the floor the day my father left, when I was seven years old. She yanked the photos out of their vinyl album pockets, making sure to cut straight into the middle of his face on each image, throwing them all over the living room floor, like weeds thrashed and ejected from under the relentless blades of a lawn mower.

I learned to never ask questions about my story because Ah-Ma always shouted the breath out of my questions as I sat frozen with chopsticks in my hand, feeling as small as a kernel of rice sticking to the rim of my bowl. "What does it matter anyway?" she hollered at me. "Your father left, and that's the end of that. Why are you asking? You wanna pack your bags and go live with your father?" Her eyes narrowed into me, like the scissors in her hand.

This was the moment I immigrated to a different kind of land, leaving my broken past behind, so I could start over. I wanted to be just like my mother—a 17-year-old, pregnant bride, who climbed a metal stairway into a Pan Am airplane to fly from Hong Kong and start a new life in San Francisco Chinatown.

Except the ocean I wanted to fly across wasn't a body of water, but oceans of broken memories and unanswered questions that silently filled the pages of my life. I tried to hide all these questions away because the new land I endeavored to enter and belong to was the land of the unbroken and the beautiful. And there was no room for baggage on this journey.

• • •

I felt this same way when I became a mom. I had finally made it. I had stepped firmly into this new land to create the family I always wanted. My weird family history wouldn't taint the new pages of my children. I felt the excitement of starting fresh, shaping lives from the beginning. My transformation into living as a normal, unbroken grown-up was about to be complete.

Once I got married, I never returned to Chinatown. I threw away my Canton-pop CDs and stopped speaking Chinese. I learned to cook pasta and stopped making Chinese bone-broth soup. I filled boxes with all the Chinese knickknacks I owned and drove it all to Goodwill. I became Mrs. Bonnie Gray, hoping that Bonnie Sook-Wah Lee would never come back to haunt me or my good life. I swore I'd never return to Chinatown. Ever.

• • •

If you've ever baked chocolate-chip cookies, you've seen a recipe that tells you to "bake for 8 to 12 minutes or until golden brown." That last part always stressed me out. What exactly was golden brown? But somehow, on the fourteenth time I peeked into the oven to check if they were ready, the hot air brushed up to singe my face, and I felt it in my gut.

It's time.

That's how I felt about my story. I was a stay-at-home mom who had just started blogging when my second son, Caleb, was born. I was writing about safe topics, sharing inspirational thoughts about the life of faith. Just like all Christian bloggers do. I was following what everyone else was doing, happy to have a part in encouraging others.

I even entered a short film contest because I was curious if I could win. It offered a thousand dollars to the person who could tell a real-life story best in 90 seconds. As I searched my mind for something unique to help me stand out, my thoughts kept returning to seven-year-old Bonnie. Of course, I couldn't tell *that* story, so I sanitized and submitted it.

I thought I had a pretty good shot. After all, how many people in the world have a mail-order bride as their mother? But I didn't win. The guy who held a multiday vigil to get a senator to sign a bill to feed children in Africa won.

It was hard to get back to writing on my blog. As I was showering, driving, or sometimes staring off into space, the question sat there.

Why don't you tell your story?

Been there, done that in 90 seconds. Can I just move on now? I wished I hadn't entered the contest.

That same week I lost, I was rummaging through paperwork, looking for my oldest son Josh's birth certificate. It was time for summer school, and I was collecting all the needed documents for him to attend preschool. That way I could get a breather while baby Caleb napped and three-year-old big brother was cutting construction paper and making popsicle-stick art for a few hours.

I opened up an old, dusty file cabinet we store in the corner of the closet, covered by piles of clothes. I was hoping I did not misplace Josh's birth certificate, shoving it somewhere random, because four years ago is a long time during baby-survival years. My fingers were traveling through the files, when they stopped on a yellowed, folded paper. I made a mental note to get this messy pile of stuff organized one of these days and opened up the document.

```
CERTIFICATE OF LIVE BIRTH
Name of Child: First Name: Bonnie
City of Birth: San Francisco
```

It was my birth certificate.

I don't think I had ever really studied the information on my birth certificate. I had used it a couple times—mainly to prove my identity, birth date, and citizenship. You know, to get a driver's license, passport, and whatnot.

But this was the first time I *really* looked at it. Line by line.

```
Place of Birth: Chinese Hospital
Street Address: 845 Jackson St.
Age of Mother: 18
Residence of Mother: 1042 Jackson St.
```

I had to read the two addresses again. Did I read this right?

I was born in a hospital on the same street as the house my mother lived in...that *I* lived in? I was born in a hospital literally called "Chinese Hospital." Where and why in the United States could a hospital be named by a race? Apparently, there is one such hospital. I was born in it.

I thought the story I had told in 90 seconds was done. But when I took a second look, I realized my story was actually just at the cusp of turning golden brown. The afternoon I found Josh's birth certificate, I folded up my own and placed it back in the envelope.

Just like I know when it's time to take the cookies out, I knew I had to take a trip to Chinatown, to find the home I was born in. I'd never had any interest before now. *What's the point?* I recognized this questioning voice. It was seven-year-old Bonnie who had learned to be invisible and be quiet. But something new sparked in me. Curiosity.

My mother and father left San Francisco when I turned five, moving us inland to a small town. Two years later, they would divorce. I had not been back to San Francisco since I married Eric. I had never seen the house I was born in.

Before I could talk myself out of it, I called our babysitter to watch the boys that weekend. I was about to do something I had vowed never to do, and I needed my husband, Eric, for this mission. Although I did not know what I would find, I decided to set my GPS for *845 Jackson Street*—for the very first time.

> You yourselves are our letter, inscribed on our hearts, known and read by everyone…you are a letter from Christ…written not with ink but with the Spirit of the living God, not on tablets of stone but on tablets of human hearts (2 Corinthians 3:2-3 BSB).

 ## LETTER TO MY YOUNGER SELF
Your Story Matters

Beloved,

Don't hide your story. Share your story. What God has done in your life…that's what you need to shine. You're the only one who can tell His story in you.

Your story matters. You matter. You are beloved.

How do you tell a tale you've wanted to forget and leave behind? You've always told yourself, *The past is the past. There's no point in looking back. Let's just move on.* But the past isn't something to be erased. It's a beautiful story God shapes to show what it means to be human and to be loved. Even when your past has made you feel insignificant, small, and not quite good enough.

God doesn't want you to kill your stories. He wants to take you where you've been and show you He was there. God wants to show you He saw the loneliness in your eyes and the tears that went unshed. When you can't put the pieces back together again, let Jesus gather them with you, so He can tenderly fold your hand into His and gently hold you close.

Everything broken that is loved becomes beautiful by His touch. Jesus sees what others have missed—how lovely and lovable you are. He treasures each broken, beautiful moment in your life because you were there.

Jesus loves you through your story, the bitter memories made sweeter by the knowledge of His presence. We all have a broken, beautiful story that makes each of us unique and real. It's how God whispers, "Abba" into the world—through loving us in our story.

The parts of the story you want to cut out are the very parts that God want to shine His beauty through.

OPEN YOUR HEART

Chinese words originally began as a drawing of what the artist first saw. The Chinese character for *heart* 心 (*xin*) can be visualized as a pictograph that shows little brushstrokes creating the image of the heart, beating and alive with movement.[1] The word *heart* is special because it is used to form the phrase for "happiness" 開心 (*kai-xin*), which literally translates as "open heart."

What a beautiful picture to embrace. We weren't designed to close our hearts to our sorrows and our joys; we were made to open our hearts to God and each other, to display the unique brushstrokes of all of life's experiences as indelible imprints of God's story.

Reflect and Share

- *What was your childhood home like?*

- *Do you have a desire to kill off any part of your story?*

- *If you gave yourself permission to be curious about your past, what would you want to know?*

Chapter 2

The Silk Dress

F orty-five minutes.

That's how long the drive was going to take from the burbs to San Francisco Chinatown. The weatherman said it was going to be hot. So I wore a summer halter dress—something cheerful and happy. But I also knew better. San Francisco is Fog City, baby. If you get a chance to go, here's a tip: Always bring a light jacket. No matter what the weather channel tells you.

The weather changes on a dime, even if you look out the window and squint because the sun is shining bright. Because far in the distance, behind the golden mountains cradling the bay, the fog is quietly collecting over icy Pacific waters. Before you know it, the skies turn gray, the chill finds its way through your scarf, and you'll find yourself walking out of a tourist trap, wearing a chunky sweatshirt stamped with SAN FRANCISCO in large letters across your chest.

I punched *845 Jackson Street* into the car GPS and hit "OK."

Please proceed to the highlighted route, it directed.

Everything was set. Except I wasn't sure if I was ready to return to Chinatown. Ah-Ma had me running from that place my whole life.

"Remember where you came from," Ah-Ma often told me. "That's where you'd still be—speaking Chinese and bad English. You would have been a *nobody* if it hadn't been for me."

Ah-Ma made the decision to move us out of Chinatown because she didn't want me growing up speaking with an accent. Her dream was that, one day, I'd grow up to buy us a home and be like other Americans.

Where we were living was just a place to stay. Not home. Home was always out there somewhere. It didn't occur to me growing up, but what Ah-Ma said was pretty ironic. After we moved inland to Sunnyvale, a small town surrounded by orchard fields, we still made a biweekly trek back. We'd drive 45 minutes into the city to pay for parking, walk up and down the hills of Chinatown, buy and lug our Chinese groceries in plastic bags, see our Chinese doctor, and buy our Chinese medicine. All while speaking only Chinese.

The new neighborhood we moved into was just as ethnically diverse. Ah-Ma was right—I didn't hear Chinese at the laundromat, drugstore, or playground. Instead, I grew up hearing kids speak Spanish and Filipino, while speaking only Chinese at home. I was the only Chinese in my grade level from kindergarten until sixth grade. My friends were Eduardo, Jerome, Jocelyn, and Delia.

So, I grew up split. To the outside "real" world, I was American Bonnie. American Bonnie was the cheerful girl playing hot lava tag at recess in first grade, geeking out with the speech-and-debate team at lunch in high school, calling teachers my friends. But the minute I stepped through the doorway back home, I was Chinese Bonnie.

Inside our four walls, I could've been living in Hong Kong for all I knew, speaking Cantonese (a dialect originating from Guangzhou, southeastern China), throwing a wok cooking Chinese food, binging on shrimp chips and Chinese TV shows. Chinese Bonnie was a quiet girl who walked her younger sister Mei-Mei home after school and opened the refrigerator door to find a carton of milk, bok choy, tofu, and half-empty shelves that smelled of fermented black beans to begin prepping dinner later that evening. Chinese Bonnie read books under her covers with a flashlight at night, until the hurtful words Ah-Ma hurled toward her that day faded a little more with each page turn. I was never Whole Bonnie anywhere.

With each mile, the freeway rolled past, taking me closer to San Francisco, I was transported to a different place and time, leaving grown-up Bonnie—who lived in Silicon Valley and spoke college-accented English and was the mom of two boys—in my rearview mirror. The little girl who walked along the slanted streets of Chinatown awakened in me.

Walking through Chinatown as a little girl often led me to visit the tailor's dress shop with Ah-Ma. My mother worked as an embroidery seamstress when she first immigrated to America, earning scraps of money sewing beads into intricate shapes of peonies, white cranes, and—my favorite—peacock feathers on cheongsams. A cheongsam (or *chi-pao* as pronounced in Mandarin) was a body-hugging, one-piece Chinese silk dress, custom-tailored for women in well-to-do society. Ah-Ma walked to the tailor's dress shop to pick up orders, and I went with her.

The shop smelled musty, and the floor was confettied with stray threads. The stern-faced man in the shop looked up with a nod to acknowledge us as we entered. He turned over beautiful folds of silk and satin cuts of fabric, stacked side by side, with dirty, dry-cracked thumbs that should never touch anything soft or pretty. He would look at me sideways and say, "No touch," shaking his finger at me like a stick.

The corners of the shop were dimly lit, but when the sunlight streamed in from the windows, falling onto the bolts of shiny fabric, blossoms of color and beauty glimmered. While the man was busy chatting with Ah-Ma, I would reach out my hand and feel how smooth—like petals to a flower—the ornamented designs embossed on the fabric felt to my fingers.

Back home, I'd see the silk dresses laid out on the sofa, catching the warmth of the remaining daylight. They were spread out next to Ah-Ma's embroidery needles and bags of plastic beads lined up across the coffee table, sprawling to the floor in a full array of pinks, purples, pearl whites, and iridescent crystals glittering in silver and gold. When the light hit, the assortment of shiny, disc-shaped sequins cast shimmering patterns onto the walls of our dark apartment.

Ah-Ma worked on many dresses at a time, placing them side by side, each in different stages of progress. I'd gently run my fingers over each one, tracing the applique of sequins expertly sewn like jewels, stopping where Ah-Ma pinned her threaded needle, like a bookmark placed where the work of her fingers paused. When my mother wasn't looking, taking a nap, or cooking in the kitchen, I'd run to stand in front of the hallway mirror, carefully pull the fabric up to my chin, and pretend I was a beautiful model, standing up on my tippy toes. I always wondered when I would get to wear a cheongsam of my own, just like one of the special Chinese ladies. Once, she caught me trying a dress on.

"What are you doing? Take it off." A minute ago, I had thought I looked utterly fabulous, sashaying left and right. My cheeks flushed with embarrassment.

"Your dress is so pretty, Ah-Ma."

"You look cheap." You could only wear a cheongsam well, Ah-Ma told me, if you had quality—what she called *hay-jut*. Without this special *it* quality, I would only end up looking cheap in a dress.

"Do I have hay-jut?" I asked.

"Have to see. You talk too much. Hay-jut all gone."

My mother never really explained how you actually got hay-jut. This elusive quality of worth was something I had to earn, to be worthy of wearing something so beautiful. Beauty wasn't something I already possessed, but something I needed to prove existed in me within the eyes of another—in someone else's estimation.

I can't say for sure, but this might be the moment I crossed out the word *beauty* from my vocabulary. I could easily see beauty in the lives of others—the way they looked, spoke, and lived. But the word *beauty* did not apply to me.

As I internalized my mother's critical words about my appearance, I wasn't trying to be self-loathing. I learned to be content without being beautiful. I didn't need it. This is how I learned as a little girl to hope for safe things. It was easier to close my heart and be functional, fulfilling a goal, performing and meeting other people's expectations, than to believe something beautiful could be seen in me.

This way of life is lonely for the soul. I was numb to delight. I worked hard to gain comfort by people-pleasing—being smart and useful, rather than feeling joy or beauty. And I came to see my story and my cultural heritage the same way. My home. My childhood, my memories, my face, my body, my clothes, our living room filled with used, mismatched furniture passed on to us, our kitchen covered in faded wallpaper, and my crooked teeth because we couldn't afford braces. My life just felt ill-fitting.

As I remembered standing in front of the hallway mirror long ago, lowering the exquisite silk dress which I no longer felt worthy to lift into view, God was inviting me to pick up the unfinished folds of the stories in my life again. Being unfinished didn't make me less beautiful, just like the dresses laid across the sofa were lovely even in their unfinished state. Each dress was custom cut to fit the woman it belonged to—measured for her every curve and embroidered with her unique design. What if my life, however unfinished, or different from another person's life, was beautiful simply because it was my life, the one God gave me?

God was showing me that the masterpiece He was at work creating in me was both unfinished and beautiful. God was bringing together the different fabrics in my life that I viewed as ill-fitting and was clothing me with His love and acceptance, embroidering my unique quirks and personality to custom fit His grace into my life, to show His handiwork.

I began to remember how soft the silk felt in my hands. I remembered how my favorite cheongsam, embroidered by my mother, glowed as I tried it on: a pink silk dress emblazoned with an opalescent, sequin-embroidered peacock, whose magnificent feathers flowed from waist down to hem, shimmering as they caught the light as I moved.

I remembered I once felt beautiful.

I thought I was disqualified from beauty, but it has always been there. I just didn't look for it. I had forgotten that part of myself, but God did not forget. Among the broken pieces of my heart, God saw beauty.

As I pictured the little girl in me standing in front of the mirror wearing the pink dress many sizes too big, I saw Jesus there beside me in the quiet. I felt the gentle touch of God's hand on mine. And for the first time in a long time, the little girl in me remembered that she once had believed she was beautiful. The sound of her tears came softly, like the gentle trickle of a running creek you happen upon unexpectedly on the day the winter world becomes awakened by spring.

• • •

It's funny the things your brain chooses to keep in the memory banks from childhood. So many random pieces left over. Right now, the memories I've carried like missing puzzle pieces seem random. Randomly happy and randomly sad.

I remember a long set of stairs—wood steps, dark and steep—in the first doorway I was carried through and later walked up.

I can still feel the smooth, cool porcelain bottom of the bathtub that stood on four legs, with a rubber plug I'd yank off with the chain.

I can never forget standing in that dark, musty closet in the hallway, feeling dust in my throat.

I remember…

Momma. The one I call Ah-Ma.

Dead. That's what Ah-Ma said I was to her. I was as good as dead to her the day I stopped being the daughter she wanted. I stopped coming to Chinatown after that.

I turned off the freeway at Fourth Street in downtown San Francisco. As the car rolled into the parking garage at Kearny and Clay, the eastern border of Chinatown, I prayed I wasn't making a mistake.

Please, God. Whatever it is I need to find, help me find it…

Our Father, we are the clay, you are the potter; we are all
the work of your hand (Isaiah 64:8).

LETTER TO MY YOUNGER SELF
You Are Worthy of Beauty

Beloved,

You don't have to hide your beauty. You are your own kind of beautiful.

There are no rules to beauty, because what brings you joy, peace, and comfort is unique to how God designed you to see beauty. Someone may have said you weren't worthy of beauty. They were wrong.

God is making something beautiful in you. *God sees your beauty.*

Your life is like a lovely silk dress, free to embroider the way you choose. You don't have to look or act like anyone else or fit into any mold to make a beautiful life.

Your loving Creator made you an original.

KINTSUGI—GOLDEN REPAIR

Kintsugi is the Japanese art of repairing broken pottery by mending it with gold. Each piece is made more beautiful and valuable for having been broken. Gold isn't used to hide flaws, but to highlight them. The breakage is treated as a valuable part of an object's history to accentuate and treasure, instead of something to disguise and camouflage.[1]

The artist embraces flaws as a way of not only repairing broken pottery, but also as a means of transforming it into something new: *an original, unable to be duplicated, work of art.*

You are God's original work of art. Allow God to be the golden repair that lovingly holds you together, filling every crevice in your heart to bring new life, beauty, and wholeness.

———————————— **Reflect and Share** ————————————

- *What would you tell your younger self about her beauty?*

- *What were the voices that first imprinted what beauty meant to you? How do you relate to the word beauty in relation to yourself? Your life?*

- *What brought you beauty as a child? How can you bring more beauty into your life today? How have you tried to fit yourself into a cookie-cutter mold?*

Chapter 3

The Candy Store

I couldn't tell you the names of the streets I walked as a child.
Don't need to. I can describe the Tetris-like enclave by broken curbs, open doorways, souvenir shops, and the Hunan, Szechuan, and whatnot restaurants lining each street. Many of the buildings now showcase new paint jobs, but one characteristic doesn't fade: history.

The Chinese Hospital was built in 1925. The hospital was constructed to replace the Tung Wah Dispensary—the original medical building—after it was destroyed by the 1906 San Francisco earthquake. The San Francisco Chinese Hospital is the first and only hospital in America named after an ethnicity.

I was first spotted on this planet in that building. Parts of me have been destroyed by emotional quakes in my life, where my heart has crumbled to the ground. But these seismic shifts weren't the kind that registers on a Richter scale. I didn't know what I'd find once I got there. But it was important to me to stand in the doorway of where my story began.

It was time to rebuild who I was and will become. To make sense of my life, I needed to see as much as I could of the past. I prayed to look back with fresh eyes.

A part of me has always believed that the past already happened. So, why go back?

This time, God prompted me to see differently. *You've missed seeing Me in it. Let Me fill in the blanks.*

Yes, God, I said. *Tell me what I need to know.*

• • •

As I walked out of the Portsmouth Square parking garage, I reoriented myself and headed up the hill. If you ever go there, you'll walk the same streets I took that day. The narrow alleyways are still there. Just as they have been for over a century.

Walk one block up the hill. You'll be standing at a very important street corner, under a pagoda-shaped stoplight. Voilá. You've placed yourself smack-dab on Grant—the Main Street of Chinatown.

Glance over your left shoulder, and you'll see your reflection against the window into one of my fondest childhood memories. You can't miss it. The green, black, and orange tiles that decorate the walls are still loud and brassy. The shop sells touristy souvenir junk now.

That doesn't matter. This will always be my candy store.

There's a lot of bad press on candy for kids nowadays. Too much sugar fries the brain, causing interference with neurotransmitters responsible for meltdowns. In other words, sugar causes kids to spaz out. Offer a kid candy, and you'd think I was offering them a cigarette. But all kids live for candy, don't they? I loved that stuff. I loved crunching on it, chewing it, and lodging it inside my cheek until half my tongue and teeth turned cherry red.

Whenever I got my chance to buy candy, it was always a toss-up between a lollipop or a roll of Life Savers candy. Life Savers usually won out. I figured Life Savers last the longest because there are so many flavors, and they take a long time to melt in my mouth.

As I stood in front of the shop window, I thought of Yeh-Yeh. My father's dad. I remembered his smile. Yeh-Yeh spoke mischief with his eyes in a way that ended in a chuckle, like he had something hidden in his hands behind his back.

I didn't get to see him often. He was sick, I think. Always resting in his room. Sometimes, he'd call out to me. "Baaawww—nnneee!" His bedroom door would creak open, and I'd know to go in.

He would hug me the way I'd imagine a bear would pull in a jar of honey, pressing me into his soft, flannel-buttoned shirt. He'd plant a wet kiss on my cheek, and I'd feel his scruffy whiskers. His hair was never combed, and it made him look funny. The good kind of funny.

After a hug, he'd pull out a lollipop, just for me. He would tug the plastic wrapper off, and sometimes it would take great effort on his part and a lot of patience on mine, because the lollipop had sat in his pocket too long and melted onto the wrapper.

It was worth the wait. I'd pop it in my mouth. He would laugh, and so would I. Then, I would leave his room just as quickly.

I never saw Yeh-Yeh after my parents split up when I was almost seven.

•••

When I was little, I didn't go to preschool. My preschool was TV. One thing I learned from watching TV was what a grandpa ought to be. Now, I know Andy Griffith was Opie's dad, but he seemed more like a grandpa to me. A grandpa would look like Andy, taking kids to his special fishing hole, sharing stories of how he fell in love with Grandma.

At school, my friends would return from Christmas break sharing how their grandpa showered them with gifts or took them camping, taught them how to whittle or do something outdoorsy. The grandpas in movies always had some wisdom to pass along that you could put on a Hallmark card—about work, family, or honesty, because they fought in a war or walked to school in the snow with holes in their shoes.

As I got older, I'd hear about grandfathers showing my friends a pathway to higher education, paying for college tuition, leaving them an inheritance or land—even taking care of the down payment for a home as a wedding gift. Or leaving a legacy of faith.

I always felt left out whenever these stories were told. I was definitely happy for my friends to have such an amazing blessing in life. It just wasn't part of God's blessing for me.

I only have two memories I can recall of my Yeh-Yeh, and they seemed of little consequence. I remember the sticky lollipop in his shirt pocket, and I remember this candy store.

As I walked inside the old candy store, I was brought back to my only other memory of my Yeh-Yeh, because after we moved away from Chinatown, Ah-Ma refused to see my father's family. There was bad blood with the in-laws I can't get into.

My mother didn't want me visiting my father's side of the family. She told me they were uneducated, redneck country folk. She didn't want me to be influenced by them, although during times she was unhappy with me, I'd be reminded I had my father's DNA.

A couple times a week, Grandpa would come out of his room and walk over to the hall closet to grab his coat and put on his wool cap. Yeh-Yeh was talking me out! We'd slowly walk the sloping streets together, hand in hand, step by step descending rolling hills of sidewalk to make our way to the same corner candy store each visit.

Yeh-Yeh would tell me I could pick out one candy. I'd make my pick and stick my arm out to show it to the candy store owner at the cash register. Grandpa would greet the cashier with *How are you?*, take out a dollar bill, and pocket his change. Then, together we retraced our steps back uphill, one hand holding onto Grandpa's, and a roll of Life Savers firmly gripped in the other, half-eaten by the time we got home.

Yeh-Yeh died shortly after my parents separated. I don't remember how my dad got Ah-Ma to agree to let me attend, but maybe Yeh-Yeh's funeral was cause for a cease-fire between sworn enemies. My father picked me up one morning to take me to my first Chinese wake. I wasn't allowed to go to the burial, but I attended the ceremony where the family burnt incense, paper money, and paper gifts to send Grandpa off to the other side.

Relatives took turns bowing and paying their respects to Yeh-Yeh, so they wouldn't be harassed by his restless spirit. Because I had already started going to church and believed in Jesus, I told my father I couldn't bow down to anyone except God. Instead, I simply stood with my hands folded in prayer to Jesus in front of the Lee ancestral altar. I paid my respects as everyone wailed around me, their fists full of tissues as the incense swirled in the air.

As I stood there in front of my grandpa's black-and-white framed portrait, his hair smartly parted to the side, combed with Brylcreem, my father whispered something in my ear I have never told Ah-Ma or anyone since: "Yeh-Yeh asked for you when he was sick. He said, 'Where is Bonnie?'"

As I stood there in the candy store now as an adult, where the rolls of Life Savers once captured my attention, my heart began to drop and ache inside, heavy and thick, swirling with emotion because I was remembering.

I miss Yeh-Yeh.

I waved Eric over, holding him close, as a waterfall of tears and words poured through. But I did not feel ashamed that I only had this one memory of Yeh-Yeh. The sound of my grandpa's sandy laughter breaking out across his handsome, boyish grin and sparkling eyes suddenly burst into Dolby stereo surround sound in my heart.

I heard my grandpa's beloved voice once again. And I recognized the forgotten familiar peace of his warmth. It told me there was goodness in the world, and I was a part of it.

I wish I could tell him I missed him. I wish I was there at his bedside before he passed away, so I could gently wrap my arms around his neck and say, "I'm here, Yeh-Yeh. I love you."

As I wept in Eric's arms, my heart was filled with gratitude, not sadness. I was thankful. Even though I had discarded it, because it seemed too insignificant compared to the stories my friends told of their grandpas, it had never left me. This one, intact, special moment remained: I was someone's granddaughter once. I was loved.

I was surprised at how crisp and rich that memory came alive as I stood there—a grown-up woman—all five feet of me. It didn't matter that the moments were fleeting and few. I felt a streak of joy and warmth. I recognized this feeling. I didn't understand it then as a girl not-yet-seven, but I know the word for it now: *cherished.*

Standing there, staring at plastic Golden Gate snow globes and toy cable cars lined up on display in the store window and now sold in place of candy, I realized something. History can be rewritten. God can fill in the blanks.

I didn't expect the past to look different. I didn't know how to rebuild. But God does. He is the soul's architect. And He's not just a commercial, retail, mass-market architect. He will take pieces and relics of crumbled buildings and reuse them to give the new building He's designing a sense of history. So that when it's erected, the new building—your soul and mine—will show character. And we will all marvel at its uniquely composed splendor.

God will send people to cross your path—sometimes briefly to touch your life, sometimes for just a moment—to let you know you were seen. Noticed. Cherished.

Those special moments might appear commonplace. But God knows how to reach you. He quietly brings a breath of goodness into your life in the way you need it most, even if you were unaware of it at the time.

There are no throwaway moments in your life. With every moment that you felt loved, God uses those pieces to preserve something pristine and true about you.

• • •

I turned to wait at the stoplight at the street corner. The walk sign flashed on. I stepped out to cross the street and made my way toward Jackson Street.

The early morning sunlight rose behind the cityscape, peeking through a motley crew of East-meets-West architecture—pagoda rooftops, shop awnings, vertical hanging shop signs, and fire escapes. The city was coming alive. So was I.

They will utter the memory of your great goodness, and
will sing of your righteousness (Psalm 145:7 web).

LETTER TO MY YOUNGER SELF
The Little Things Matter

Beloved,

It's okay to feel deeply about the little things that give you joy. Your emotions make you human, not a burden. It's important to honor the moments you feel are special.

Move toward the people and experiences that help you feel there is goodness in the world and in you. Whatever you do, no matter how small, embrace what makes you different.

Cherish the little things that matter. They will become treasured memories. The length of time someone who cared for you spent with you doesn't make a memory less beautiful or less yours. It might have felt too brief to be significant, but it holds great value because someone once imagined what would bring you joy and comfort. And you opened your heart to receive that love simply.

You may not have a family legacy to celebrate, but your Heavenly Father carved a legacy of love into your soul through the simple memory of someone kind He put on your path. Picture your Heavenly Father turning toward you through the comfort of a listening ear, a hug, or a hand that reached for yours. Hear Jesus whisper, *You are worthy of time spent together. You are important.*

You don't have to be rich or do something Instagram worthy to leave a legacy of love for the people in your life. Your presence is your gift. Your inheritance will be the memory of your voice and laughter. The memories you create will feed their soul. There will be goodness in the world because for one moment, you paused and spent time with someone, not as they should be, but just as they are.

ADAPTIVE USE ARCHITECTURE

Adaptive use is an architectural term for the repurposing of properties that embody historical or cultural significance. An old Army warehouse could be converted into an art museum; an abandoned church could become a unique restaurant.[1] Taking this design approach to our own lives empowers us to see God's artistic eye, as He builds His signature style of love into the history of our lives, expressing His artistry across different cultures, economic landscapes, and families.

God is an innovative architect who doesn't build cookie-cutter strip malls. God preserves the history you've lived to create a one-of-a-kind life, using your unique experiences, personality, and humanity. God repurposes everything to make all things new.

You are God's most important building. First Corinthians 3:16 (NKJV) asks, "Do you not know that you are the temple of God and that the Spirit of God dwells in you?" God is using all the little moments in your life that seem quirky and out-of-place to show He is walking through life with you.

Life becomes richer when we build on the diversity of our shared experiences. The truth is, we are simply walking each other home. We don't have to walk alone.

Reflect and Share

- *What would you tell your younger self about the importance of the ordinary, little things?*

- *How is God inviting you to renovate your life to make it more you? What is something simple that gave you peace or joy in the past, and that you can share to bless others today?*

- *What is a special memory you have with your grandfather, grandmother, aunt, or family member that is significant to you?*

Chapter 4

Strange Medicine

I love playing tour guide to San Francisco whenever friends visit from far away. I don't know if it's because people enjoy having me lead them around, or whether I enjoy feeding them random bits of information. I'd like to think it's the former.

It's a lot like marketing, really. I remember what Donna, the first female manager I met in my new job out of college, told me as I was about to give a presentation at some schmuck-schmuck meeting. I was an engineering project manager working in IT, leading a kickoff team meeting at Wells Fargo Bank. We were deploying the first nationwide online banking system in the industry in the early '90s, giving customers the ability to access their bank accounts through a website.

I chose to wear a black pencil skirt that day and matched it with a '90s wrap blouse and a bright smile. I guess I still looked nervous because Donna pulled me aside before the meeting to say, "Don't show them how scared you are. If all you know is just a little more than the person sitting next to you, you can call yourself the expert in the room!"

That's why I like taking people to visit a Chinese herbal store. Before you take one step in the doorway, your nose starts to twitch. A cocktail of roots, shrubs, and goodness-knows-what-else wafts through the air, and your brain does a 180. It doesn't even know what hit it.

The smells of a Chinese apothecary shop are, literally, downright foreign.

If you've ever taken a whiff of Tiger Balm, you'd know what I mean. It is a powerful, superminty, pungent ointment to soothe muscle aches that Costco now sells. It comes in a large tin that's so big, it's ridiculous. So I wouldn't bother pointing out Tiger Balm to you. You already know about that.

No, if I were to take you there, I'd walk you up to the shop I frequented since I was pint-sized. It's crazy to still see the shopkeepers. The short, weatherworn, stocky shopkeeper's wife who can easily throw her husband over the top rope in a World Wide Wrestling match is still unpacking boxes and taking inventory.

Her husband, a big-belly man sporting a receding hairline that reached to the back of his head, still sat on a stool at the back counter, grinding herbs and slicing ginseng with a guillotine trimmer. Whenever I walked in with Ah-Ma, the shopkeeper broke out his cigarette-tinted smile and welcomed me with a bellowing "Hah-low, Loi-Loi!" (*Hello, little girl!*) that made the unfortunate hair growing out of the mole resting on his upper lip jump like an exclamation point.

I liked the shopkeeper very much. He was always so happy to see me. It felt strange to bring someone so much joy when I didn't do a thing except show up. The shopkeeper dried his own raisins and folded them into little packets, making tiny envelopes with white paper like origami. You would quickly unfold it later, after you drained the last horrid dreg of herbal medicine, gobbling something sweet to counteract the insanely bitter taste in your mouth. The shopkeeper always slipped me an extra packet of raisins before I left, which felt like I was holding sunshine in my pocket. I'd pop a few in my mouth to enjoy on the walk home.

The shopkeeper and his wife appeared tinier than I remembered, and the store entrance narrower. They looked older, a bit more wrinkly, but not too much—surprisingly unaged, like old Yoda appeared in *The Empire Strikes Back*.

One thing hasn't changed. The wall of herbs looked exactly the same.

The herbs are kept in small drawers running from floor to ceiling that pull out, like old-school card catalogs in libraries past. As a child waiting for the apothecary (who was the shopkeeper himself) to fill a prescription, I'd sit on a stack of unpacked shipping boxes and stare at the wall of drawers. Unhurried and steady, the pharmacist methodically curated the appropriate ingredients, opening and shutting some drawers, while bypassing others. He shuffled, as if in a trance, reaching up, down, and across the boxes, like a mechanical arm in a jukebox.

What was even more mysterious was the Chinese doctor's writing on the prescription itself. It was a swirl of Chinese characters written vertically top to bottom on letter-sized white paper, right to left, a cross between doodles and ancient art, inscribing a combination of healing remedies that the apothecary decodes.

Everything was so Chinese. It was all very familiar to me. But it was also so very strange.

I've taken both Western and Chinese medicine. Western medicine is sweet. It's covered with cherry, peppermint, and grape flavors.

I took plenty of penicillin back in the day. Back then, pediatricians dispensed it like Infants' Tylenol today. Enough to stain my baby teeth. I can still picture bottles of the stuff in the fridge, next to the carton of milk. Ah-Ma walked me over and put a cold spoonful in my mouth. One swallow and all gone. If you don't think about it too much and imagine watching an episode of "Looney Tunes," it's over quick. Short and sweet.

Not Chinese medicine. No, the Chinese boil their herb very, very slowly. An hour minimum, simmering leaves, berries, twigs, and crazy stuff that stinks up the whole house. The sicker you are, the smellier it gets. You know you're in for it when you hear your mom hollering because the medicine's bubbled out of the pot, spilling into the drip pan.

Didn't matter. You still had to drink it. Three cups of water boiled down to one. It was poured black into a rice bowl. Sometimes it was so black that you got scared even looking at it. I'd whimper, claiming it was way too hot. Mom would blow on it and let it sit a bit.

But Chinese herbal medicine needs to go down warm, while the molecules are still in motion. Heat penetrates the healing deeper, I was told. Chinese people believe if you don't eat food or drink your soup hot, while you still see steam rising, you'll miss out on the life-giving energy it releases to nourish the body. Reheating leftovers once might be okay for lunch. *Maybe.* But reheat leftovers twice? You might as well be eating Styrofoam. It's been stripped of all goodness.

To get the bitter medicine drink even near your lips, you must hold your nose. I learned that bitterness is good: The more bitter the taste, the more effective it is at killing whatever's ailing you. When I was very sick, and the healing I needed was deep, I learned to look into a cup of darkness and willingly open my mouth to drink it in.

There were limits, though, to home herbal remedies. One time, in third grade, my cold and cough were especially bad. I know now, as a mom to two boys, that what I had was probably Hand, Foot, and Mouth Disease, because sores broke out all over my tongue, mouth, gums, and throat. My head burned with a fever that left me as limp as a wet noodle.

I needed to see a Western doctor; I needed antibiotics, and I needed money because we didn't have health insurance. I'll never forget standing in the parking lot, staring at the entrance of Tao Tao Restaurant, where my father now worked as a waiter. Ah-Ma drove me there and told me to ask my father for money to see the doctors. Whatever I came down with had infected my younger sister. Ah-Ma told me not to come back to the car unless I got the money from my dad.

I hadn't seen my father for a long time—not since he stopped visiting and left us. So I was nervous about seeing him again. What should I say when I see him? Ah-Ma didn't give me any pointers.

I stepped into the lobby of the restaurant, ringing the bell hanging on the door on my way in, and waved down one of the workers.

Sit there. I was pointed to one of the red vinyl chairs lined up against the wall for customers waiting for to-go orders.

Would my father be happy to see me? Did he look the same? Just as I nervously wondered, he appeared, more jostled than me.

"What is it? Why are you here? You shouldn't have come through the front door. It's for customers." His eyes looked troubled, trying to find the next words.

"I'm sick…" I croaked, swallowing hard from sore tonsils, and awkwardly blurted. "I need some money to see the doctors."

"Tell your mom I don't have any money to give her! Go. Tell her!" He looked angry, placing one hand on the small of my back and the other on the door handle to push me out.

I started crying. Crying because I didn't know what to do. Crying because I couldn't go back to the car without money to help my sister and me. Crying because I was afraid of my mother as much as I felt shame filling me, from my head down to my feet.

I turned around to say, choking through tears, unable to stop everything messy from pouring out of me without a Kleenex, "Ah-Ma said I can't go back," I sputtered like a car with dead batteries. "…unless you give me some money."

My father reached into his back pocket and opened his billfold. I felt sorry for him. I didn't want to take his money.

He counted some bills, folded them in half. As he stooped down close to put the bills in my hand, I could smell the mixture of gel, cigarettes, and sweet-and-sour pork in his hair.

He led me out the door, looked straight into my eyes, and said, "Never come here to ask me for money again. Okay?"

I fought back my tears and nodded. I made a vow that day walking across the parking lot to get back into the car. I vowed to never ask him or anyone else for money ever again.

I made a vow to never need anything from anyone ever again. From that point on, I would grow up and make something of myself, so I would never be in need. I vowed to care for my sister and Ah-Ma, no matter what the cost. I wobbled away, swallowing my tears and drinking in the black bitterness down my throat.

● ● ●

There were dark and strange days lived within the walls of my childhood.

I didn't want to be different. I didn't want memories nobody else seemed to have. I wanted my life to look and smell like candy, sweet and happy. But my life was more like living behind the walls of an apothecary, where my ability to swallow the hard, bitter moments was my modus operandi. I began living under a different set of rules from normal people. I drank in my role of being the provider for my family wholeheartedly. I was like Thomas the Tank Engine, who just wanted to be useful and trusted that it all served a purpose.

I believed once I finished the cup of suffering handed to me as a child and built a life to make up for all the lack, having taken care of everyone, everything would be better when I grew up. But this feeling of being different never got better. *When will I belong?*

As I stopped to take pictures in the apothecary shop, surrounded by the familiar props of my childhood, overcome by memories, a peculiar awakening dawned on me. I was not the only one coming back to visit this shop of wonders and mysterious ginseng, chrysanthemum teas, and honey nectars. Someone else was sitting next to little Bonnie on those old, crumpled boxes decades ago.

I didn't notice Him or know His name back then. He sat there so very quietly. But I realized, zooming back in time, this someone sitting on boxes with me at the apothecary was also sitting next to little girl me on the red vinyl chairs at Tao Tao Restaurant, as I was waiting to see my father.

Jesus. Jesus was there beside me, His tears falling as His heart broke in a thousand pieces right along with mine, as I walked out the door and it swung shut behind me, with cash in my hand. He was drinking in my bitterness right along with me, to the very last drop. He tasted my painful memories, dark and lonely. Jesus was there with me, holding a bitter cup of blackness in His hands, just as He did in the Garden of Gethsamane. Because one dark night long ago, He too collapsed onto the ground, shaking and in tears, overwhelmed and sweating drops like blood, as He asked His Father, "Will You take this cup from Me? I don't want to drink it. Is there any other way?"

There was no one to comfort Him either, as Jesus chose to drink the bitter cup of rejection that battered His body, as He hung on the cross and wounding words rained down on Him, like daggers onto His soul by the very people He loved the most. Unlike me, Jesus did not yield to the shame. Jesus yielded to the pain. He drank the brokenness in, all the way to the last drop. Jesus willingly did this because when He looked in that dark cup of shame, He saw the little girl in you and me. He did not want us to drink the bitterness in life alone, so He drank it with us.

Jesus drinks the bitter cup of loneliness, so our brokenness is made beautiful because He loves us in our lonely hour of need. He loves us in the moments that once broke us, so we don't have to hold on to the vows we once made long ago to rely on ourselves and no one else. We can let go of the vows to stay strong but lonely because Jesus folds His loving hand in ours instead. It is time for us to open our heart to heal and be loved instead.

Jesus loved me faithfully. He didn't change my situation, but He protected me from letting it poison my heart. Pain is what I've been through, but it isn't my name. I am God's beloved, and so are you. God has been loving us all along.

We can let Jesus take the cup of brokenness from us. We can loosen our fingers and choose a better way. Let us come to Jesus with open hands and open hearts, like jasmine tea petals softening in the warmth of porcelain teacups, buds opening to release its sweet fragrance, blossoming fully in the present.

I thanked the shopkeeper for letting me take pictures. I didn't want to cry. So, instead of asking, "Do you remember me?" I said, "Thank you for the pictures. Have a nice day."

I was getting closer to my destination of the Chinese Hospital, but I decided I would take a detour instead. The journey was paved with unexpected discoveries. I was no longer afraid to linger. I wanted to wander a little more.

Strange medicine indeed.

> I led them with cords of human kindness, with ties of love.
> To them I was like the one who lifts a little child to the
> cheek, and I bent down to feed them (Hosea 11:4).

LETTER TO MY YOUNGER SELF
You Are Worth Loving

Beloved,

You are not alone. You are loved.

It's okay to feel lonely sometimes. You don't have to hide your wounds. We all need someone.

Suffering isn't shameful. Being in pain isn't brokenness. It's being human. You are loved for who you are, not just for what you can offer. The people who really care about you don't feel burdened by your needs or feelings.

When you stop hiding your flaws and embrace them as gifts of vulnerability, you see that life doesn't have to be perfect to be beautiful. Brokenness is the doorway to intimacy. Brokenness allows you to let others in.

Don't compare your pain. Honor your pain. And know that you are worthy to be loved, just as you are, this very moment.

THE ART OF TYPOGRAPHY

Typography is the art and technique of arranging, setting, and designing type (letters) to make words readable and appealing. The world's first typography with movable type printing technology used to print paper books was invented in China during the Song Dynasty (AD 900–1051), using character tiles hand carved out of porcelain. Six hundred years before Gutenberg, Chinese monks used a method known as block printing, coating wooden blocks with ink pressed onto sheets of paper, to produce the earliest forms of written language in poetry, stories, and history.[1]

You are God's living artwork, His new form of typography. You are God's newly designed, unique font that the Master Graphic Designer created to convey a new beauty and aesthetic. God deftly arranges the typesetting in your life—the time, people, places, and memories—to form pieces of the beautiful stories God wants you to share with the world.

Reflect and Share

- *What would you tell your younger self about her wounds of rejection and loneliness—and how she is worth loving?*

- *How is God redeeming the past and using it to grow new things in your life?*

- *What are vows you once made to yourself, and how have they shaped who you are today?*

Chapter 5

Bookstore

Although I hadn't gone back to my childhood home since our family moved away when I was five, I recall it was a four-bedroom flat by recounting the members of my father's family with whom we lived. Yeh-Yeh (my paternal grandpa) and Mah-Mah (my paternal grandma) shared their bedroom with Fifth Uncle (he lived with mental disabilities and required close care). Then, there was Third Uncle, his wife, and their daughter, my cousin Serena, who took residence in another. My aunt Gu-Gu occupied the third room. My father, Ah-Ma, and I lived in the fourth bedroom.

Once a week, First Uncle (my father's older brother) and Fourth Uncle, along with their families, descended upon the flat to gather around a table and eat a big Chinese family dinner. In total, there were 16 people in the Lee family. There was always too much food, with dishes crowded so closely together that the table looked like a completed Othello game board—all pieces loaded, no spaces. You had to sit a few feet away so you could fit more chairs in, although the venerated elders of the family got the best spots. The table seating was prime real estate, and the rice bowl and a pair of chopsticks in your hand was your place setting. My cousins and I sat at the kids' table, where the most coveted prize was snagging a roast duck leg.

In sync with the massive amounts of food emerging from the kitchen was a heap of family politics—easily rivaling today's reality TV shows because Ah-Ma would tell me all the dirty laundry of who had done what to whom and why. Ah-Ma was just 18 when she immigrated to the United States, becoming a new mom with a husband she hardly knew. So I can understand the temptation to make me her surrogate BFF.

Ah-Ma insisted that we mainly stay in our bedroom, saying, "I don't want you growing up redneck like your dad's people." We came out of our room when it was near mealtimes, when Ah-Ma helped with the cooking.

To avoid her in-laws as much as possible, Ah-Ma took me for a daily walk through the streets of Chinatown. Our routine was unlike a preschooler's routine nowadays—a trip to the children's museum, a picnic at the park, or maybe a Gymboree class for music enrichment. No, my preschool days were spent as Ah-Ma's companion going to her favorite places.

One regular stop was a shop located on a side street on Waverly Place. The door swung open to a bell's ring, and Ah-Ma and I would step into rows upon rows of white wooden shelves across the floor and lining the walls. My mother's favorite place was a bookstore.

To me, the bookstore was more art gallery than shop, with the most popular books displayed face out. As Ah-Ma quietly flipped through potential picks, taking some off the shelf to scan the back cover like an archaeologist studies rocks, I found the quietness among books a soothing respite, like walking through a redwood grove.

Our apartment and the eclectic urban city surrounding it broad-casted a continuous cacophony of noises—a spontaneous combustion of commotion made by trolleybuses dragging their electric poles across a spiderweb of wires and workers hollering above the boom of pallets of vegetables being plopped onto hand trucks. Mix in the fiery rumble of cable cars hurtling past—along with the sound of the gripman throwing levers down, operating the clutch of a 15,000-pound car lunging passengers downhill—and boom! We had surround-sound living in a town that hardly ever slept.

But there in the bookshop, walking between rows of dust jacket designs, I entered into a sacred sanctuary, away from the noise of our intergenerational living space and the city itself.

I loved the smell of books like I love the smell of summer in Montana, when you drive up a mountain road with your windows rolled down to catch the scent of wild sage blowing west, as the afternoon melts into the evening sky. I loved the way pages turned when a book was crisp and new, the weight of it resting in my hands, like the reassuring clasp of a childhood friend's hand when you jump double Dutch and find yourselves magically skipping rope in the air together. The world felt weightless and happy at the same time.

Books were my first friends.

I was five years old when I heard my first book read to me in English. My kindergarten teacher, Mrs. Carol, wore her hair in a soft '70s bob flipped to one side, and a happy smile that shimmered like her frost-blue eye shadow, matching her satin blue scarf and cream-colored turtleneck. She sat down in a big chair on the first day of school in front of the classroom, as we all sat on the carpet, crisscross applesauce.

As she lifted the big picture book that rested in her lap to open and crease its pages back, I wondered how she managed to hold something so big in one hand. As she began reading the lines to "Twinkle, Twinkle, Little Star," the text floating across the page framed by illustrations of a painted night sky and stars in vibrant colors, the words welcomed me. My heart was filled with something beautiful—something that has never left me to this day as I read and write.

I felt loved. I felt joy. I felt everything wonderful and bright. In between the pages as they turned in Mrs. Carol's hands, I felt that I belonged.

Like the North Star, words tethered me as I morphed between my Chinese and American worlds. Whenever I felt lost, I would read a book. As I turned the pages, I felt parts of me coming together. I felt a little more whole, reading someone else's story. Because what I experienced could be named, I existed, and I was real.

I grew up poor, unable to afford to buy much. But the one thing I possessed without cost, like auburn-colored leaves falling in autumn to adorn my walk home from school, was the companionship of a friend, speaking to me through the voice of the author on ink and paper. A library was like a clearing in the forest, and the books lining the shelves were the friends I would go meet to spend the day together.

I belonged to myself a little more each time I read. As I did, I was able to be both broken and whole, Chinese and American, traveling safely between the opposite worlds of poverty and riches. Words were my home.

The bookstore of my childhood was a Chinese bookstore. I waited patiently for Ah-Ma to browse because after we left with her book in a brown paper sleeve bag, we would walk down the street to a second bookstore. There I would pick up a Chinese version of *Highlights* magazine called *Yue Toong Lok Yuen* (Happy Childhood Garden)—a collection of stories, featuring comic-strip illustrations of a blue robot cat named Ding Dong Doraemon and his adventures. My favorite pastime wasn't playing with dolls (though I loved my Raggedy Ann doll), but making up my own stories based on pictures I saw as I flipped through the magazine, because I couldn't read Chinese.

One day, I asked Ah-Ma to teach me to read and write Chinese. So, while I was learning to sound out English words watching Rita Morena, the cranky film director on *The Electric Company Show* on PBS, scream, "Hey, you guys!" one of the first books I owned was a thin Chinese workbook with block-lined pages stapled together, where I practiced writing my Chinese characters. I wrote in Chinese before writing my ABCs.

Little did I know that this love of storytelling would someday be used by God to heal me of childhood trauma, when panic attacks began to grip my body, sending me choking, unable to breathe, as I curled up into a ball every two hours.

•••

Some months after I returned from Chinatown in search of my childhood home, I was contacted by a literary agent, offering to sign me on after he came across my book proposal.

I had started a blog nearly by accident a year before, when I needed a nonbaby outlet as a new mom of two boys when Caleb was born. Eric set up a blog for me so I could archive my journals while the baby napped. Little did I know my blog would gather a following, and I'd end up with a book contract.

It was a childhood dream come true to become an author. But one weekend in winter, when Eric surprised me by booking a cabin in the woods to give me dedicated writing time to work on my manuscript, I finished the first ten chapters and stepped out to walk up a hillside, only to fall into one of the most terrifying, traumatic treks in my life.

My heart started racing. Then it started pounding. My chest tightened. My throat started narrowing. The sky turned white, and my entire world became oversaturated with light. I couldn't see. I started feeling dizzy, then nauseated. I wouldn't have been so alarmed if I hadn't started gasping for air. Choking. I fell to the ground as I struggled to breathe.

That night, unable to sleep, my body became flooded with feverish chills. Hot flashes. The next day, after writing another chapter, walking on the same path, it happened again. What was wrong? When I returned home to get checked out and have tests done, the doctors found I was healthy, and I was even more at a loss.

I finally reached out to a therapist who was the founder of a Christian counseling center in Silicon Valley. As I described my symptoms, Dr. Patterson said, "Yep. This is a classic case of PTSD."

PTSD? *That can't be right*, I thought. I wasn't ever a soldier on a battlefield. "Did you know that emotional abuse—verbal abuse—has the same impact as physical abuse?" Dr. Patterson asked.

"But no one is hurting me. Why is this happening now?" I didn't understand. "Everything's good. I have a great husband. I'm happily in love, married, with two beautiful baby boys. I'm fortunate to be a stay-at-home mom. I have lots of friends, and I have a very close relationship with God. My faith is strong," I added, because I felt ashamed that the therapist might think otherwise. What he said next sent shock waves through my soul.

"Well, a soldier doesn't experience anxiety or panic attacks when he's out on the battlefield," Dr. Patterson explained. "He is being strong, fighting to survive. He's busy helping, taking care of others. Getting things done." He paused so his words would sink in. "When does he experience panic attacks?"

"When?" I took the bait.

"When he comes back home," Dr. Patterson answered. "When a soldier is safe, and he has returned home, his body is finally able to experience the trauma he could not at the time it was happening, when he was busy fighting, surviving, and taking care of others."

As it turned out, what I was experiencing on that dirt path was a panic attack—a symptom of post-traumatic stress disorder. Yes. Me. The girl who had never been afraid of anything, was about to embark on a journey to heal from childhood trauma.

"This is happening, not because your faith is failing. It's the opposite," Dr. Patterson assured me. "Your faith has helped you overcome hard things. You've done good. Your nervous system automatically blocks what's too overwhelming at the time it's happening. It's God's natural protection designed to protect you when you were a child. Now, it's time for healing. This is homecoming."

This was earthshaking truth—the-world-is-not-flat, life-changing truth. I finally understood, and I began to cry.

Apparently, my anxiety wasn't about something bad happening to me, but about something good? I was coming home. Now that I was safe in a loving relationship, and my dream of becoming a writer was coming true, my body and my heart could finally experience the emotional trauma that I could not earlier in my life.

All these stories I had put away behind the steel trapdoor of my heart were not supposed to be thrown away. They were key to my healing. Behind each story I'd put to the side that made me feel like I didn't fit in, didn't belong, wasn't loved—behind each story was the little girl who longed to be accepted, celebrated, and loved back to life.

I was being invited to embrace everything that made me feel different about myself, to celebrate what I once viewed as flaws as doorways to my humanity and God's loving presence. Because these parts made up my true worth: the unique person God created me to be.

Your voice matters.

Your story matters.

You matter.

Your story has value because you have value.

To heal, I needed to relive the stories I thought were leftovers—just bread ends only useful for throwing out to feed the pigeons. I was wrong. God was transforming my bread ends into manna falling from the sky to heal my soul. My soul was being fed with God's love, as I made peace with my past. Not by putting the past behind me, but by embracing it in the present as brokenness made beautiful.

When the apostle Paul said, "Forgetting what is behind and straining toward what is ahead" (Philippians 3:13), he wasn't talking about erasing his past. Paul was referring to forgetting his old way of life as a Pharisee, turning away from focusing his worth on how things appeared and on his spiritual performance. Paul was no longer training to lead a life unmarked by brokenness; instead, he was "straining toward" knowing Jesus intimately, by sharing in the truth of "His sufferings, being conformed to His death" (Philippians 3:10 NKJV).

There is grace in the wilderness. I know this because even in the desert, God speaks. As the prophet Jeremiah told us, "The people who survived the sword found grace in the wilderness" (31:2 NKJV). God makes a roadway in the wilderness, streams in the desert. Like Elijah who heard God in the quiet aftermath of a fire and an earthquake, I heard God's gentle whispers of rest emerge out of my life of trying hard to fit in: *I am here. You are Mine. You are My beloved.*

With God's loving whispers guiding me, speaking into every wound, I began healing.

As I did the hard work of healing my emotional traumas, the panic attacks, anxiety, and depression gave way to sorrow and grief—and then to a deep, abounding peace.

Spring was here.

Although the wall of snow and numbing cold might have once kept you safe, locking your hurt from the rest of the world, one day you'll see that spring always comes. You were made for spring. You will see your tears become a river of healing peace.

> This is what the Lord says: I will make peace flow to her like a river (Isaiah 66:12 HCSB).

LETTER TO MY YOUNGER SELF
You Are Worthy of Healing

Beloved,

Your emotional well-being is so important. Honor what you've survived and overcome. Honor your journey.

Don't feel guilty for needing care. Be proud. You've done good, girl. Now, it is time to take better care of you. Prioritize your soul care, nurture, and healing.

Healing your heart may be the most powerful act of faith God is calling you to make today. Take care of that little girl in you. Seek out a therapist—an expert who has experience guiding others through the wilderness of memories.

Your story is worth remembering. You are worth valuing. Be curious. Let God love you. Take the intimate journey of healing. You'll be amazed by the beauty and be transformed by it.

THE ANCIENT ART OF
BOOKBINDING IN CHINA

The invention of papermaking by the Chinese in AD 121 led to replacing silk scrolls with the folded leaf book. One of the earliest known techniques of paper bookbinding is "butterfly binding," developed in the ninth century When you opened the book, the shape of the book leaves resembled the wings of a butterfly.[1]

So it is with the healing journey. As you allow God to love you deeper, you move from being a pamphlet of faith, to opening your heart like beautiful butterfly wings to God's loving touch on every page of your stories. Though you were once wrapped in a protective cocoon of grace to survive the hurt you sustained—so you could be strong and overcome in the moment—you weren't meant to live in this numbed state your whole life.

There will come a time when God will tenderly meet you in those hard chapters of your life so you can awaken your soul to rest and break free. The metamorphosis is taking place where others see only inactivity. Yet, God is at work with might and power.

Reflect and Share

- *What would you say to your younger self about taking better care of herself?*

- *What are ways God's calling you to take better care of yourself physically or emotionally?*

- *What were your favorite books as a child? What stories did you enjoy reading?*

Chapter Six

Noodle Shop

It was getting toward lunchtime. It was time to find a place to eat.

Being in Chinatown, it's a no-brainer what we'll eat. It's time for noodles. Having noodles for lunch is like stopping for sandwiches to Americans. Chinese people grab a bowl of flat rice noodles prepared by a crusty-looking cook. He's wearing a crinkly folded white hat and nursing boiling pots of water laid out over a tic-tac-toe grid of gas ranges, donning an apron splattered with food that looks like a Chinese Jackson Pollock painting in the kitchen.

Don't let this scare you. It is evidence that this restaurant is legit. The wonton noodle cook's apron is like a canvas for a painting. A great, delicious bowl of noodles is a work of art. The noodle cook uses a wok spatula for stirring, a spider skimmer for blanching noodles and Chinese broccoli *gai-lan*, and a ladle to transfer the broth. You'll see the noodle chef move in an energetic dance—pouring, whisking, and splattering—over his canvas of noodle pots, dipping into finger bowls to sprinkle in spices and chopped green onions, filling dozens of orders in frenetic motion.

His gaze never strays from his beloved noodles, throwing them up in the air with a skillful flick of his wrist as they land in a savory, steaming, beef bone broth soup. With graceful motion, he drops in crunchy, sweet shrimp meat wrapped in silky dumplings for protein. To complete his work of art, he adds a few sprigs of green bok choy leaves, quickly zap-cooked with a few swishes in maddeningly hot, boiling water for vegetables.

Add a few pinches of fresh cilantro with some red vinegar, chili sauce for dipping, and all is right in the world. If you're eating with a few friends, be sure to order a plate of beef chow fun and a creamy, glassy bowl of Sam Pan congee (Chinese rice porridge) so you can share everything and enjoy it family style. Instant bliss.

Watching such noodle-cooking artistry was like watching a magic show, and as a little girl, I was absolutely mesmerized by it. Wiry-thin waiters carried up to four of these jumbo-sized noodles soup bowls on one tray, like an acrobat balancing plate stacked upon precarious plate.

I admired their hard work and grit, and I always thanked them saying, "Mm goy!" even though they replied with a grunt, if at all. In time, as they saw me come in regularly, they smiled, welcoming me like a long-lost niece. I appreciated the attention and care poured into something simple that was so delicious, joyful, and comforting.

Eric and I backtracked to head to my favorite Hon's Won Ton Noodle Shop. It's a hole-in-the-wall place where businesspeople in smooth, crisp suits trekked in from the city's financial district to sit elbow-to-elbow next to disheveled everyday citizens with weathered faces. Side by side, men and women slurped noodles between bites of tender, braised beef stew, some taking a break from collecting aluminum cans, while others escaped their cubicle offices to grab a bite to eat.

I felt oddly comfortable with both extreme slices of socioeconomic lives across the table from me because I had grown up poor and eaten here alongside men with shiny watches and women in high heels. Later, as a new college grad working in corporate high tech, I walked here from just a few blocks away to pick up my chopsticks and eat here too.

Enjoying good food is the unifying bond of kinship. During lunch hour, when it's standing room only with a long waiting line crowded at the door, you share a tiny four-person table with strangers sitting across from and next to you. There's no such thing as personal space, so just tuck the bowl of noodles in front of you like a flamingo lowering its head down into the water to feed.

It was between bites of noodle soup that it dawned on me: *My father was a busboy working in a noodle shop, just like this one here.*

• • •

The last visit I had with my father doesn't fit any father-daughter category of what others might find beautiful. But it is a treasured memory that still warms my heart to this day.

My father picked me up in his olive-green Nova with the black, peeling rooftop at Ah-Ma's house to spend the day together. But instead of going to McDonald's to get a cheeseburger like we usually did, Bah-Ba drove me to his apartment across town, next to the county social services building.

His apartment looked like a motel with its black shingles, flimsy like the soles of an old pair of shoes. I followed my father up the cement steps, and after a few wobbly shakes while turning the key, he opened the door to his new place.

It felt odd to step into his single-room studio apartment. An uncovered mattress for a bed lay on the floor in one corner, and a chair propped up next to a card table stood on the other side of the room. His vinyl suitcases and Chinese newspapers sat on the floor next to a dusty TV with really long rabbit-ear antennae and nothing much else.

Bah-Ba asked me if I was hungry and said he would make me a sandwich. He went to the kitchen countertop, took out two pieces of white Wonder Bread, popped them in the toaster, and placed them on a paper plate. Then he opened a short plastic fridge. It was empty inside except for a pack of butter, a jar of Smucker's strawberry jam, beer, and a box of Arm & Hammer baking soda.

He peeled the wax paper back from a stick of butter and proceeded to slice four thick squares of butter like it was ham and arrange them on one piece of toast. The slices of butter were so thick they didn't really melt into the bread—just enough to stick. On the second piece of bread, Bah-Ba spread a gob of strawberry jam.

He put the two halves together and cut the sandwich into two triangles. One for him and one for me. And that is how my father made me my first solid-butter-and-jam sandwich. He poured me a cup of water from the faucet, and together, we stood at his small kitchen counter and ate our father-daughter lunch.

My father smiled, lifted up his triangle half sandwich, and said, "Ho mei!" which translates as "Good tasting," as if to say "Cheers!" I didn't want to be rude, so I giggled a little in reply, to encourage myself to bite into this strange sandwich.

But you know what? It actually tasted good, and I thought it was fun to eat. I never had one-on-one time with my father since he worked six days a week—Chinese restaurant hours—which meant he was gone in the morning by the time I woke up, and I was asleep by the time he came home.

● ● ●

This is my one memory of my father making breakfast for me, and it makes me happy to relive it with you. Though I never told anyone about this, I thought my father looked rather adorable making me something to eat. Because he was happy making it, it made me happy watching him make it.

This is something I remember so powerfully that it became an important touchstone for me when I became a mom myself. If my boys see me happy spending time doing things that make me happy, it is going to give them happiness.

So, while I don't have memories of my father like my other friends do, of their dads eating PB&Js with them, making pancakes, or barbecuing on Memorial Day, this memory is mine. In one place, for one moment in time, I was someone's daughter. And we were happy together.

Just the two of us. It was a moment when my heart was unbroken. I belonged, and I was whole.

God lived that memory with me as it happened, and He is holding your hand in your memories too, sweet one. He tenderly whispers: *Safe here in My arms. I am your home.* This memory of belonging was neither part of my American nor my Chinese culture. This was a moment belonging to our human culture.

Now, as a mother myself to two boys, whenever I'm feeling a bit down or the kids need a pick-me-up, I take out the bread. I put four slices in the toaster and open the fridge to take out the butter and raspberry jam. I turn on the faucet to boil some water and make a pot of peppermint tea. Josh and Caleb know it's time to take a break.

We gather to sit at the kitchen counter and enjoy something simple but delicious together. My boys will know who I'm thinking of when the aroma of melted butter and jam and fresh toast wafts through the room. I am remembering the little girl in me who was happy.

That little girl in me who is being restored is sitting next to the little boys she calls her sons, creating memories of her very own with them. We are creating a place of belonging with one another. One day, they will look back on their memories, and the seeds of love I am planting will blossom like a field of wildflowers, pointing them to the peace God whispers to them in this broken world. They will be reminded they are beloved.

> By day the Lord directs his love,
>   at night his song is with me—
>   a prayer to the God of my life (Psalm 42:8).

LETTER TO MY YOUNGER SELF
You Are Worthy of Finding Your Voice

Beloved,

I know you feel the need to hide different parts of yourself. You grew up in a family that looked different from everyone else's, so you're used to shifting what you say or do to blend in.

But when you try to please everyone, you end up losing yourself. There is space to be you in this world. Let others know what you really like, what you find funny, strange, or sad.

I promise you, when you are honest about the weird things that make you happy, you'll finally find the belonging you so desperately long to be a part of.

You'll become part of the human race, like Jesus did when He came into a world that didn't fully understood Him, to let you know you are not alone. You belong to Him.

JADE: ROYAL GEM

In the history of Chinese art, going back to 3,000 BC, jade—known as *yu*, the "royal gem"—was considered more valuable in the East than gold and in the West than diamonds. The most valuable kind—"imperial jade"—is known for its vibrant, emerald green hue and high level of translucency and is even said to glow. This rare jade is formed when the rocks are subjected to high heat and intense pressure over time to create intricate crystals. This process only occurs in metamorphic rocks, which start out as nonprecious. But under pressure, over time, they become transformed into precious gems.[1]

What a beautiful picture! As you become more transparent about who you are and your struggles, you reveal God's beauty forged under intense pressure. Through hardship, God releases the vibrant colors of your unique personality, perspective, and life experiences. By shining a light on your pain and joys, you release God's beauty to glow in your authenticity!

Jade is covered in a hard rock crust. To the untrained eye, the true value of the gem may go unrecognized, even causing the gem to be discarded. But God sees your worth, and He wants you to celebrate it too. God whispers, *You are beautiful. You are My precious gem beyond value.*

Reflect and Share

- *What would you say to your younger self about how to find belonging?*

- *In what ways is God inspiring you to find belonging and connection with others?*

- *What are the different worlds you live in? What is a memory you have of feeling happy with your mother or father? That moment is yours.*

Chapter 7

Vegetable Stand

To get to the hospital, we passed through Stockton Street. This is where all the shopping for fresh meats and produce happens daily in open-air markets lined up at attention. Storefront canopies stand at salute, then flap in the wind like open arms, waving people in.

The farmer's market doesn't happen just once a week here in Chinatown. Grandmas, who could double as running backs on a football field, battle it out daily with wiry-strong moms balancing babies slung in carriers to pick out the best water chestnuts, Asian pears, and cuts of oxtail. This cluster of humanity swarms the fruit stands like bees on a honeycomb.

It's the busiest street in Chinatown, so you cannot be shy. Be bold to push your way through, but still maintain decorum. Walk leaning in at a slight angle, so you lead with your shoulder like the bow of a boat cutting through the waves of people.

Stockton is where Ah-Ma and I trudged to buy groceries every day because with ten people at the dinner table in an intergenerational family gathered in a small space, there's no way to squeeze enough food in the fridge. This street is our Main Street, where commerce intersects with what Chinese people value most: family, joie de vivre, and food:

fruits, produce, seafood, and meat. And not just any food. This food must be *fresh*.

Food is so fresh—directly transported from farm to produce stands—that as bok choy, shiitake mushrooms, and carrots tumble out in piles, shoppers start combing through the goods before they're even sorted or organized. Workers continuously stack crates on the side, jumping off double-parked delivery trucks to beeping horns of impatient motorists. Seafood isn't shrink-wrapped, but dumped swimming into tanks—shrimp heads with black, pinhead eyes and long antennae intact and moving. Fish still alive and jumpy are laid on crushed ice in open barrels, so shoppers can check for freshness.

I learned to check for freshness as a little girl, watching Ah-Ma poke her finger into a googly-eyed orange rock cod to make sure the skin bounced back, pricking her fingers across the scales to confirm they were tightly attached. And the final test? Lift the gill to check if it's pink underneath. Make sure its eyes are bulgy and shiny. Then, pick that fish up even if it's flapping and put it in your plastic bag. Later that night, you'll have that fish steamed with julienned ginger, light soy sauce, and diced scallions. I did feel a bit sorry for the fish, gasping for air. But I soon forgot it when enjoying chopstick bites of fish, sweet and tender, later that night.

Grocery shopping with Ah-Ma was such a big part of my daily routine as a child. But some of my most cherished days unfolded when I found myself unexpectedly spending time with Po-Po. My grandma.

• • •

After Ah-Ma became a U.S. citizen, she emigrated her family—my grandparents, three uncles, and two aunts. It took five years for the paperwork to be processed. When they arrived, my grandparents were very hardworking. While my grandfather Gung-Gung worked six days a week as the fry cook at a Chinese restaurant at the mall, Po-Po ran a little home daycare, taking care of babies and toddlers, up to three or four at a time.

Truth be told, I was drawn to my Po-Po because she was the person in my life who praised me whenever she saw me. "You're such a smart girl!" Po-Po would declare. She hugged me as often as she paid me compliments. The person I remember giving me hugs as a child was not Ah-Ma, but my grandma.

"Help Po-Po go get groceries?" Grandma asked me with a sparkle in her eye, and we would walk to the neighborhood market together. "If you help Po-Po push the cart back, I'll give you some peanuts!"

I don't know why peanuts were such a big attraction in her mind, but I was happy to help my grandma because she shopped for seven in the family, and on days when my younger sister and I stayed with her, we made it nine. I knew money was short because Po-Po and Ah-Ma fought over whether we could bring laundry over to use the washing machines and how much water we were using up. The conflict between my grandma and Ah-Ma wasn't really about laundry, but deeper mother-daughter issues. Eventually, the dysfunctional accountings of who-owed-whom-what estranged my mother and my grandma, which kept me from seeing Po-Po for many years.

I wanted to do my best to help my grandma. That's a lot of heavy groceries to push home through the crossword-patterned path of sidewalks. I opened up plastics bags ready to receive her produce picks and bag them with twist ties.

"Don't pick the long, skinny ones," Po-Po told me, teaching me to pass over green beans that were tough and stringy. "The shorter, round, fat ones are tender and sweet."

Side by side, like water cranes stabbing their beaks into the water for the day's catch, Po-Po and I picked out the good beans and bagged our treasure trove. She'd tell me to run cold water over them briskly after blanching them so they stayed crunchy. Later, I'd help Grandma wash and snap the beans, then watch her cook the beans before transferring them from wok to colander for a quick rinse in the kitchen sink, then throw them back in for a final, yummy stir-fry with sliced chicken.

I pushed the shopping cart home, while Po-Po walked next to me shelling peanuts, passing them to me like magic beans. I'd pop them in my mouth and ask her questions about growing up in China as a little girl.

My grandma told me she and her family had to run away from their village during World War II when the Japanese were bombing their homes. They had nothing to eat. Tears would fall and a sad look clouded her eyes, as she recounted how she only had a few grains of raw rice to eat, and how her baby sister wouldn't stop crying because there was nothing to feed her. Po-Po and her family escaped to the countryside as planes flying overhead attacked. Over 20 million Chinese were killed during that terrible war, and my grandma was a survivor.[1] Of course, I also tried to get a romantic account of how she met Gung-Gung, but Po-Po just laughed, "We don't think about stuff like that!"

I was in third grade when Grandma and I did these walks together—the same year my parents divorced, resulting in my loss of both parents in different ways. Ah-Ma went to work six days a week, working crazy hours stir-frying beef and broccoli at a Chinese restaurant, never home. I was left on my own, spending my days shuttled between places. It was the year I lost my childhood. I became an old soul.

• • •

During one night at Grandma's house, waiting for Ah-Ma to pick me up past midnight, I got very sick. I was coughing so hard that I couldn't fall asleep. It was the kind of spastic cough that squeezes the breath out of you so badly, you wish you could throw up, hoping it would break the cough's choke hold on you.

I started crying; my head hurt. I stared so intensely into that empty, dark room that I started seeing blotchy shades of blackness I didn't know existed. I was like an astronaut floating in outer space, without a comm link back to earth.

"I'm all alone," I whispered into my pillow drenched with tears. I unraveled the toilet paper roll I kept under the covers to blow my nose. We didn't use Kleenex because it was expensive.

As I staggered my breathing to stem the cough, I felt a gentle hand on my shoulder. I turned to see who it was in the dark.

"Po-Po," I croaked through my messy tears.

"What are you doing, crying in the dark?" She smoothed my covers, whispering, "Mo hom la." *It's okay. Don't cry.*

Grandma tore more toilet paper from the roll and wiped my tears. "Good girl."

I sat up to collapse into Grandma's arms, clutching her, weeping with relief. "There, there now," Grandma patted my back. "Lie down. Lie down."

Grandma held a miniature-sized bottle of caramel-colored liquid in one hand. She unscrewed the red top, turning it upside down to dispense it into her hands. Grandma began to soothe my cough, gently rubbing a Chinese peppermint ointment called *Po Sum On Yau* around my collarbone. Then, on my chest. She helped me sit up and massaged the balm onto my back. As a sweet, minty fragrance filled the room, I exhaled. She gently laid me back down, tucking the covers closely beside me.

"Better now?" Grandma asked.

"Thank you, Po-Po," I replied, my nose less stuffy, my eyes now heavy with sleep.

"Try to rest. If you cough again, Po-Po will come help you," she assured me with one final, extra tuck.

This is my first memory of being comforted. This was the moment I felt worthy of being loved.

My grandma's hands resting on mine felt like home. Her hands shelling peanuts, washing green beans, her arms hugging me. The comforting presence of a friend's hand is what communicates love and worthiness.

Now, I remember this every time Josh or Caleb cries at night—as babies and even now as teenagers, when they rustle me up and tell me about their growing pains, or the flu keeps them up coughing. I often forget, and my first response is trying to explain why there's a logical reason for discomfort, rather than giving comfort—telling them how things will get better in a few days, listing symptoms and diagnoses as no cause for worry, and why-don't-you-just-try-to-sleep.

But then I remember my grandma's hands. My beloved Po-Po.

I begin to soothe them, rubbing their backs, or I go down to the kitchen to make a cup of tea and bring it up to them. We sit together as they take a sip. I gather my boys in my arms, place a loving hand on theirs, and whisper, "It's going to be okay. I'm here. I will help you."

$$\bullet \ \bullet \ \bullet$$

When I first became a mother, I read books to make sure I did parenting right. I didn't know what to do. How do regular people raise their children? I didn't have a good role model and felt critical of myself at every turn, doubting myself.

But I thought back to Po-Po, marveling at how the memories of her kindness still comfort me as an adult. Then, I remind myself my worth as a mom isn't found in trying to parent like other people. My worth as a mom is found in simply being present—comforting my children with kindness, spending time doing everyday things like grocery shopping and cooking together, hugging them, and telling them my stories, just as I am.

One of my favorite scenes of Jesus has Him sitting on the beach quietly, turning fish over a warm fire, cooking for His beloved friends. He had died and come back to life. Wouldn't He want to prove His worth by showing Himself to His enemies?

Instead, Jesus chose to love His friends. Jesus cooked for them. Jesus could have turned stones to bread and had fish ready to eat in an instant, but He chose to sit by a fire and slowly, carefully tend to the fish until the skin tightened slightly, cooking a comforting meal for His friends who had stayed up all night and were exhausted and discouraged.

Come sit down, Jesus invites us. *Warm yourself by the fire. The fish is almost ready to eat.*

I see kindness in Jesus's eyes. We savor this goodness each time we show kindness to each other, when we have caught no fish and our nets come up empty. We say to each other, "There is space here for you. Come sit down. Warm yourself by the fire. I have warm bread and fish to share. Rest awhile. You are welcome here."

I remember my grandma and how good the world felt when I was next to her. I know that, one day in heaven, I will be able to do what I could not when I was a little girl. I will thank her for the gift she gave me. It's one of the enduring gifts I endeavor to pass on to my children, my friends, and the strangers I meet today wherever I may be. *Kindness.*

My world feels a little brighter, as I make my way through these streets I once abandoned. I wondered what I would discover next on my journey, feeling a little less lost and a little more at home.

> The LORD appeared to us in the past, saying: "I have loved you with an everlasting love; I have drawn you with unfailing kindness" (Jeremiah 31:3).

 ## LETTER TO MY YOUNGER SELF
You Are Worthy of Kindness

Beloved,

Don't be hard on yourself.

Be kind to yourself.

Kindness is the beautiful gift you have power to give others in this lonely world who are hungering for love and friendship. Spending time with someone is quiet, beautiful kingdom work that Jesus cherishes and celebrates. You can bless others with a soothing touch or by simply sitting across the table to listen with a cup of tea. The world needs your brand of simple kindness.

You can bless others with simple kindness that the world is too busy to make time and space for. You can change a life that will flower in years to come with the loving hand of God's comfort through yours.

PORCELAIN CHINA

The word *porcelain* is derived from *porcellana,* used by Marco Polo to describe the pottery he saw in China. Porcelain was first made in China in the sixth century. The highly coveted "blue and white" rice-grain-style porcelain bowl was developed during the Ming Dynasty and was exclusively produced for the Chinese imperial court. When you hold the bowl up to the sunlight, because of the transparency of the porcelain, you will see that the decorations intricately carved along the walls of the bowl are not rice grains, but translucent patterns of beautiful petals of flower blossoms.[2]

You are like fine porcelain china. With the touch of your hand or the soothing comfort of your voice, you will leave someone's heart feeling loved because of your kindness. They will walk around in the daylight with a heart decorated and pierced by goodness because you took the time to be kind.

Reflect and Share

- *What would you say to your younger self about being kind to herself?*

- *What are ways you enjoy expressing your gift of kindness?*

- *What is your first memory of receiving comfort, and who gave it to you?*

Chapter 8

Women in the Mirror

One of the shops you probably wouldn't go in as a tourist in China-town is the hair salon. But for me, the hair salon was a source of hope, enabling Ah-Ma to put food on the table and pay rent and clothe her two girls.

Women wearing stylish mules on their feet stood on tippy toes above customers, who were flipping through old magazines, and crouched in yoga-like poses with comb and scissors to point cut and texturize a fringe. I can't tell you how much it meant to our livelihood to see my mom become one of them.

As I entered junior high school, Ah-Ma decided to improve her station in life, when a social worker suggested she study to become a hair stylist. She enrolled in cosmetology school through a special government program for low-income families…and guess who also started studying how to do perms, cut hair, and learn the differences between shears, clippers, and razors, along with techniques for facials, massages, and a catalog of illnesses that nails fall prey to and how to manicure them?

Yep. Yours truly. Because my Ah-Ma couldn't read English, I sat at our kitchen table each week with a brick of a cosmetology textbook open, flipping through a Chinese-English dictionary to translate whole chapters, one at a time. Ah-Ma sat next to me with her pencil to write the Chinese characters on the page while I used a yellow highlighter to mark vocabulary words she needed to memorize to pass the cosmetology exam.

It was a great accomplishment that filled me with joy and pride when Ah-Ma graduated and got her license. To make money for our family, Ah-Ma set up shop by gluing square mirror tiles onto the wall of our little galley kitchen, in the space between the electric stovetop and dining table pushed up in the corner. Someone from church donated an old, swiveling desk chair, and voilá! We were open for business.

The women who came through our home for a haircut and perm were members of our church congregation. I know now, looking back, they came to support Ah-Ma and to help take care of my sister and me. Women were willing to stand over our tiny bathroom sink as we pulled the shower hose over to the vanity basin to wash their hair. If she had a perm, I would give her a hand towel to place over her eyes, so she could shield her face and avoid going blind from the chemical perm solution running down as the waterfall rinse began.

Every time a customer left, my sister and I asked Ah-Ma how much tip was left. Haircuts started out at $5 to $7, depending on hair length, and perms were $20. We always felt like we'd struck it rich when somebody occasionally left a $5 tip or a thank-You-Lord $10.

One of the things I loved about having a home salon was that sometimes a visitor showed interest in talking to me. My life was very narrow because I came home right away after school to help my sister with homework. I never got to go over to a friend's house, and sleepovers were not a part of my growing-up experience.

Because the friends in my high school honors classes lived in the nice neighborhoods—on the "other side" of the railroad tracks, in ranch houses that looked like mansions to me—I never invited them to come to our dinky duplex, with a greasy kitchen and mildew-spotted bathroom shower. I lived on one of the busiest streets in Silicon Valley, where cars and freight trucks clunked past, zooming right outside our screen door. You could hear the neighbor's uncensored conversations through our thin walls. Visiting would have traumatized my friends.

So, a visitor coming for a haircut was a special social treat. As she sat in that office desk chair, draped in a salon cutting cape in our kitchen, with her hair dripping wet, I would pull out a seat at the dining table and start chatting with her. My life was inhabited by grown-ups and, when given the opportunity, I became an instant extrovert, drinking in the chance for interaction.

As they became regular customers, I'd see them every six weeks. They became surrogate aunties, asking me about school, friends, and interests. Some of my favorite aunties (children are taught to address adult women as Auntie instead of Mrs. or Miss) brought my sister and me candy, cute pencils, or stationery.

One woman, Auntie Kitty Lam, was an elderly Chinese American woman who spoke English accent-free. I found her absolutely enchanting because she dressed like she was perpetually living in the '60s. Auntie Kitty wore gigantic green melamine hoop earrings and a jawbreaker-sized orange beaded necklace with matching bangles, and her toes were always painted fiery red, with lipstick to match. Her neck was folded in wrinkles, but her voice spoke in dramatic "ohs" and "ahs" like she was auditioning for the theater, booming with laughter and never short of a story to tell.

Auntie Kitty was one of the few professional women I met who worked as a nurse, because most customers were college students or housewives. She was a widow, and she always had some advice for me. "Read as many books as you can, Bonnie!" She'd shoot out random words of wisdom like she was passing out gumballs, as I sat there watching Ah-Ma trimming her hair. "Always speak your mind. You're an American girl!"

One time, Auntie Kitty gave me a *Reader's Digest* subscription for my birthday. Between watching Laura, Ma, and Pa on *Little House on the Prairie*, a ridiculous amount of freeway crashes on *CHiPs*, and reading the monthly *Reader's Digest*, I learned about the world outside our four walls. I scoured each month's edition, gripped by stories of surviving a tornado in the "Drama in Real Life" section, learning about office humor in "All in a Day's Work," and inhaling the book excerpts in every issue. Seeds of my dream of becoming a journalist or writer were planted. I relished stories and developed a natural affinity toward curiosity and putting people at ease by asking questions.

Auntie Kitty renewed my *Reader's Digest* subscription every year for more than two decades until the day she died. Before I left for college, she gave me her gorgeous, perfectly tailored '60s treasure: a black wool coat with pointed collars, adorned with floral buttons, that she had kept pristine with mothballs in her suitcase. After graduating from college, I wore that coat to win my first job interview in San Francisco's financial district.

After each customer left, I would sweep up the hair and clean the barber's station, washing combs, brushes, and shears, so everything was ready for the next appointment. I was filled with gratitude for welcome conversation and reprieve from the monotony of home life. Each visit was a window into life beyond our family of three.

Although they were regular customers, the women sitting in front of the mirror-tiled wall in our kitchen became angels God used to bless me and shape my worth as a woman.

* * *

One of these women in the mirror was Merrianne. She was my Sunday school teacher when I entered junior high. She had just graduated from college and, one day at church, she pulled me aside.

"I was wondering if you'd like to get together once a week," Merrianne asked.

"What would we do?" This was odd. Why would she want to get together with *me*?

"We can do a book study together."

My ears perked up at the mention of the word *book*, but I was worried. "I need to be home after school," I said. Ah-Ma *always* needed me home.

"I'll come to your house," Merrianne offered. "It's really a chance for us to chat. We can pray together. Get to know each other."

This was like winning the lottery. Because this was for church, and it didn't cause any imposition on Ah-Ma, our weekly meetings were set.

Merrianne was the only person throughout my childhood who actually came to my home to visit me and spend time with me. I still remember the first book we studied together, even though it's out of print today: *Your Worth as a Godly Woman*. I don't remember what I learned reading the book, but what I did learn about my worth was experienced through the time Merrianne spent with me. We met with each other from the time I was 12 years old until I graduated from high school at 18. I grew into a woman under the shelter of her friendship.

God loved me through Merrianne's friendship, and her mentoring and discipling me. After I left for college, we lost touch. We saw each other sporadically, like at my wedding and when my first baby was born. But when the panic attacks began, the first person I called was Merrianne. It didn't matter we hadn't spoken for years. Her response when I called crying and scared, trembling from my panic attacks?

"I'm coming right now. Where are you?" Merrianne dropped everything, and 30 minutes later I was sobbing in her arms as she held me close. She offered to pick up the kids from school every day and even fold my laundry, because there were days I could not even get out of bed from the anxiety and depression that was being released as I received healing and therapy. She took my two-year-old Caleb and five-year-old Josh to the park and museums, watching over them so I could go to my therapy sessions and take a nap afterward.

As a child, I never did trust Merrianne enough to break the taboo of revealing family abuse. I didn't tell her about the verbal and emotional abuse I was enduring. I didn't tell Merrianne about the terrible fights going on under our roof between Ah-Ma, my sister, and me—how our mom would rage at night and keep us up for hours, how I cried myself to sleep, wondering where my father was, how I worried about how we would pay the bills every month.

I didn't tell her any of this because it felt too shameful. I didn't want her to pity me or look down on our family. I wanted her to keep coming to my house. I wanted to be worth the time and effort she was investing to mentor me.

Little did I know that Merrianne would have loved me unconditionally, as she did later when I was an adult and told her everything about my broken past. God knew Merrianne would encourage me, and He placed her in my life so that one day, as a new mom of two boys, I would be able to turn to her and receive the love and care I needed to heal.

. . .

There were many more women in the mirror I met over the years, whom God used to dispel my loneliness with the gifts of friendship and conversation. Through these women in the mirror, I discovered God uses our different walks of life, personalities, ages, and stages, to enrich our lives with variety and joy. They taught me we are designed for friendship, and that life can be beautiful, even if it is hard, when we have the shelter of a good friend.

Life is a long journey, and it is a treasure to stop by the wayside and encourage each other. To share a cup of tea and conversation together. Our burdens will feel lighter.

We weren't meant to toil and journey alone. We need to feel known, seen, and valued. I became a woman of worth, not because of what I could do for these women, but through the gift of paying attention to each other. By sharing what brings a smile, we blossom a little more with each small, brief, or in some cases, big and enduring moments.

We might not have a picture-perfect family (who does?), but God provides another way. He places people on our paths to be a refuge. These are friends who become family.

Friendship thrives in the most unlikely places. Sometimes, we just need to know we are worthy of friendship in order to make space for it, seek it out, and prioritize it. It's part of our humanity. *We should never give up believing we are worthy of friendships.*

Friends are like flowers, starting as seeds planted deep in the soil of our hearts, which over time bloom to add color and beauty to our days. It might seem like a luxury to grow flowers when you are primarily focused on survival, achievement, or relational hiding. But as C.S. Lewis once observed, "Friendship is unnecessary, like philosophy, like art...It has no survival value; rather it is one of those things which give value to survival."[1]

How can we know that God values beauty? He plants the seeds of friendship to testify you are worthy of beauty. You are good soil. You are worthy of lovely things.

Sometimes it's hard to see our true selves in the mirror, but friends give us courage to be seen. And when we've lost our way and don't know what brings us joy, we can help each other rediscover joy together and heal from life's brokenness. Listening, caring, and nurturing each other's souls is the sunshine we all need to sing our song in this world.

I'm grateful these women gave me the shelter of their friendship because one day, I would need to somehow find the courage to rewrite my story by faith—not by fate.

> Your love has given me great joy and encouragement, because you…have refreshed the hearts of the Lord's people (Philemon 1:7).

 ## LETTER TO MY YOUNGER SELF
You Are Worthy of Friendship

Beloved,

It's hard to trust again after you've been hurt by friends.

For the longest time, it may even feel safer to serve others and soldier on emotionally alone. But although you want to protect yourself, you also long to trust again.

Pray for new vision for friendship, and let the beauty found in nature inspire you. Friendship, as I've come to learn, isn't a possession. Friendship is more like flowers and a sunrise; friendship is a gift to bring light and beauty as it crosses our path.

It can be painful to see a friendship go. But don't stop taking risks. Just as our souls never grow tired of hoping for sunsets, shooting stars, flowers in bloom, or art that moves us, we cannot give up on friendship.

When we open up to make new friends or to nurture the ones on our path, we free our hearts to connect with Christ. We are saying, "I see God's beauty in you."

ART OF SHU BI—CHINESE HAIR ORNAMENTS AND HAIR COMBS

In ancient Chinese culture, hair was considered an important, intimate part of the body to honor, like one's skin. Hair was worn long and not cut. When a boy turned 20 or a girl turned 15, their parents celebrated with a coming-of-age ceremony. Girls wore hairpins decorated with flowers or animals as part of this ceremony to mark their passage into adulthood, and boys wore a hair binding decoration (an ornament for their man bun).

Hair ornaments were worn by noble women dating back to the Han Dynasty in 202 BC and were made of gold, silver, jade, shell, or bone.

One of the most celebrated arts in Chinese history is wearing hair combs, called *shu bi*—a hand-painted Changzhou comb that requires 28 steps to produce the shu (comb) and 72 processes for the bi (teeth of the comb). The art of creating this comb involves carving, painting, heating, engraving, and grinding—achieving master-level craftsman skills.[2]

Friendship is a form of art as well. Nurturing a friendship takes time and creating memories together. Just like the shu bi takes many steps, friendships grow with intention, listening, and encouraging each other because we are all works of art in progress, under the care of our Master Craftsman!

Reflect and Share

- *What would you tell your younger self about the lessons you've learned about friendship?*

- *How can you be a friend to younger women? How can you reach out to find a mentor on your journey today? What hobbies or interests can you share with another woman?*

- *Who are the "women in the mirror" in your life who encouraged you to embrace your worth as a woman?*

Chapter 9

Fate

Half a mile long by a quarter mile wide.
Can you imagine how small Chinatown is? It brings me back
to the days when I was asked to run the mile in junior high for physical fitness tests. Four laps around the track. It's still how I measure distance in my head. Who says you don't learn anything in PE?

In the time it takes to circle the track twice, I will have covered the length of the world I lived, moved, and breathed into my being. One more lap to finish that quarter mile, and achievement unlocked. I had walked the breadth of Chinatown.

In the year I was born, the population of Chinatown was seven times the San Francisco average, hitting a population density of 35,000 people per square mile. That's quite a stat to crunch. The Chinese American people are resilient. We are tough, flourishing like a bamboo forest.

On a practical level, I recognized the boundaries of my childhood neighborhood by my favorite wonton noodle shop sitting at the "bottom" border of Chinatown at Kearney Street. It hugged the financial district, just two blocks over, where the second tallest skyscraper in the city, Bank of America, drilled into the ground, like one of the crystal beams lodged in Superman's crystal cave where he was born—the Fortress of Solitude.

Superman returned later as a teenager to his crystal cave to discover the truth of his real identity because the cave contained "memory crystals" to access Jor-El's words of wisdom. This was the father he never knew until he viewed his hologram. Here I was returning to this city to uncover the truth of my identity. Except, I didn't have any recorded holograms—only memories long buried, unlocked as these buildings brought my past back to life again.

Even though the noodle shop was a hop and a skip from downtown, Ah-Ma and I never stepped one foot past Chinatown. We never crossed over into the different, foreign dimension called *Sai Yun Gai,* which means "West Man's Streets." We lived in *Tong Yun Gai,* translated as "Chinese People Streets." We stayed in the box drawn for people like Ah-Ma, where she could speak the language and read the signs, where we could afford to buy what we needed. That was the world I understood, and it became the box of reality for me too.

Tourists from all four corners of the world came to visit. With cameras in hand, couples paired in matching cargo shorts plodded through Chinatown to peer through smudgy windows. Some saved for a lifetime to travel to the City-by-the-Bay and, as a side attraction, made a detour here. They snapped pictures of paper-painted fans and hand-carved jade pendants in glass displays, and they rummaged through a pile of plastic cable cars on sale for $2.99. Passing by them was a different group of travelers—people who gave up everything to breathe the air in this neighborhood.

They hurried past with solemn faces and blue-collared hands. A Chinese man brushed past in frayed clothes, cigarette smoldering between his fingers. He took a turn into one of the noodle shops and collected orphaned chopsticks and half-eaten bowls of soup and dumped them into a large plastic bucket that pushes on squeaky wheels. He is a busboy, and he could have been my father.

Immigrants arrived here with dreams brimming in their eyes, just like the 17-year-old girl who landed on a transcontinental flight from Hong Kong many years ago, pregnant. I would soon arrive by her side as her daughter. Unnamed, yet to be born.

Everyone who has ever taken a trip anywhere new on vacation has always gotten lost.

Some people even plan trips without an itinerary because they hope to stumble onto something exciting. Not me. I like my maps and travel guides, thank you.

On the occasions when I get disoriented, I try not to sweat it. I've gotten used to feeling lost. You'd never guess that I ever get lost when you see all the street signs translated in both Chinese and English, hanging side by side in San Francisco Chinatown. The streets are bilingual.

So am I.

Most people like to say I have the best of both worlds. It's a cliché that's never sat right with me. A person can't live with more than one identity without sacrificing one for the other. Without a place where they can fully belong. I've walked around with two halves of me living in two different worlds, never fully present in either. It's a bit like the children in *The Lion, the Witch and the Wardrobe,* who traveled beyond the wardrobe but could never bring Narnia back with them. Everyone around me spoke Chinese, including the people in the stores we shopped at. But when I turned on the TV, Kermit the Frog and Big Bird spoke a different language.

How does someone like me find one place where they can feel whole?

It was hard for me to explain to friends growing up that I'd gotten used to living with dual identities because being born in and living in Chinatown was like living in a different country within a country. I was balancing life between two worlds, and I often envied Ah-Ma because at least she knew where she came from. At home, I lived in one world with my family. The minute I stepped through the doors to go to school, I stepped into another world. I didn't fully belong to either, so I existed alone.

When you don't know your story, you take on the story of the person you long to be loved by most. Their stories become yours, and you embrace them as your own because it's the closest thing you have to feeling whole and finding home.

My home was Ah-Ma, and even though I didn't understand all

the pieces of her story, and even though she was only half of me, without my father in my life, that meant she was all of me. Ah-Ma was my everything.

● ● ●

I do.

According to Ah-Ma, when she made this vow to marry my father, fate plucked her up from Hong Kong—the third most densely populated country in the world with seven and a half million people living on a 426-square-mile island—to land her in the second most densely populated city in America. San Francisco Chinatown is the oldest Chinatown in North America, and second only to Manhattan in population density.

I was born in the largest Chinese community outside Asia—15,000 residents are boxed in, living within a 20-square-block radius full of one-way streets.

When Ah-Ma said *I do* to the matchmaker, my mom said she was walking onto a one-way street with no U-turns.

"Why did you do it?" I always asked, "How could you marry a stranger who was ten years older and move where you didn't know anyone or speak the language?"

"Because," Ah-Ma explained, "it was my fate."

● ● ●

Pieces of Ah-Ma's story never came complete. She never wanted to talk too long about how she came to America, and if I pressed for details or peppered her with too many questions, Ah-Ma would change the subject or get up and walk away.

Ah-Ma told her story in spurts and sputters, often in the kitchen, as I stood at the sink swish-swashing the silt out of leafy yau-choy under running water until my fingers turned icy numb. The kitchen proved to be the best place to collect pieces of her story throughout the years. Ah-Ma felt most like talking while sprinkling teaspoons of cornstarch over bite-sized cuts of chicken in preparation for a savory glaze made by mixing peanut oil and soy sauce with her chopsticks in figure-eight swirls in a porcelain bowl.

I worked as Ah-Ma's sous chef as soon as my elbows were tall enough to clear the counter, standing over a big, round Chinese wooden butcher block, as thick as a telephone book. I'd wield a big metal cleaver to chop, smash, and mince garlic with one hearty slap down. Every late afternoon, whenever Ah-Ma hollered for me, I put down my pencil to bookmark my textbook and homework, hollering back "*Lai La!* Coming!"

I hurried to chop green onions for her to throw into the wok or to quarter meat, deboning and trimming slices of beef from stubborn fat and sinew, working fast to properly fillet meat. Lost in the hum of hot oil sizzling in the wok, in the rattle of steam shooting out from a dish of succulent pork and chopped, preserved mustard greens (*mui choy* 梅菜) bubbling under the lid, my mother told her stories, hypnotized by the sounds of cooking.

"Our family had no money," Ah-Ma would tell me. "I wasn't the firstborn. I was born second. I wasn't a son. No value." Ah-Ma's voice would break like static, her nose flared and reddened, as her eyes flinched with a mixture of pain, anger, and sadness flashing across her face, like storm clouds moving across the ocean.

She told me how her grandma, Mah-Mah, played favorites, sneaking food and candy to others in the family, while Ah-Ma was told the features of her face looked unlucky and would bring ill fortune. I always stayed quiet, careful not to break her train of thought. She told her story like a script she kept reliving.

There are only a handful of defining moments in a girl's life during which she becomes a woman. Ah-Ma told me when she was 13, her mother asked her to stop going to school and stay home to help her take care of six younger brothers and sisters, a year or two apart, including a set of twin baby boys.

"You have to help me." That's what my Po-Po, her Ah-Ma, said. "All these little ones. I can't do it alone. You're a good girl. You care about your brothers and sisters, don't you?"

My mother told me that because she loved her Ah-Ma and couldn't stand seeing her brothers and sisters crawling all over the ground hungry, dirty, and crying, she quit school. "Family is most important! Without family, you have nothing!"

Ah-Ma's words were not spoken with tenderness or affection, but with biting bitterness. That was my mother's defining moment as a woman. Her worth was measured by what she gave up, to prove her love to her family.

Love was measured by how much personal happiness you relinquished. The more important your sacrifice to you, the greater the evidence of your love. My mother quit school at 13 and sold plastic flowers in a basket in the street market to help make money. "I was like Audrey Hepburn in *My Fair Lady*," Ah-Ma told me.

"What about your older sister, Yee-Ma?" I asked. *Yee-Ma* in Chinese means "second mom." Why was my mom chosen to quit school instead of her? It was the plot twist I hated.

"Because Yee-Ma was the oldest, she was favored. The matriarch of our family, Mah-Mah, my grandmother, loved Yee-Ma. But since I wasn't a boy, and I wasn't the oldest, it was my fate to quit school and go to work." My mother emphasized this next point, "You don't get to choose your fate. You're born into it."

I wanted to wrap my arms around Ah-Ma, hold her, and fill her life with everything beautiful and bright. I wanted her to see the world as I saw it from my American eyes of optimism and opportunity, full of possibility and goodness. I wanted to tell her she was wrong about what her Mah-Mah said to her. She was not unlucky. She was blessed. She was beautiful. And I would be the one to help love her until this wonderful life became her reality.

I swore to myself I would love her until all the darkness was loved out of her, like sucking the poison out of a snakebite. My love would be her beacon of light, the morning sunlight dissipating the fog in the harbor of storms that were keeping happiness from her. I wanted to see Ah-Ma smile. Because when she did, all was right and good in my world.

I wanted to be a good daughter. Because, you see, I was the firstborn of Ah-Ma's two daughters. I was not born a son.

That was my fate.

• • •

The American part of me hated knowing my mother's choice was taken from her, when clearly there was favoritism. From my years of public education and to the credit of the most amazing teachers, I grew up believing we all have the freedom to create the life we were destined to live. The pursuit of happiness is a basic human right.

Yet, something was in the air I breathed as a child in my home that did not allow me to dream of such a luxury unimpeded. Happiness like this was for other people who grew up in different families. Like the kids at school who had moms and dads sit in the audience and clap for them at winter concerts while I walked out of the auditorium alone to call from a pay phone for Ah-Ma to pick me up. I knew my reality was different, and I accepted it. I endeavored to give my Ah-Ma a better life. Family was Ah-Ma's guiding beacon in life, and it became mine.

But did I really have to choose between the pursuit of happiness and my love for my family? After all, I was both Chinese and American. Couldn't I live in both worlds? Because I was young, I still had hope. I wanted both. I never in a thousand years would have fathomed I would face the choice my mom faced when she was turned 17. Would I gamble my family for a chance to pursue my happiness?

Running from fate didn't make it go away. There will always be a one-way street to walk down, Ah-Ma told me. Right around the corner.

Out of the blue, when Ah-Ma turned 17, Po-Po told her she had been chosen to marry a stranger. She was chosen out of everyone in her family to help the family emigrate to America for a better life. A matchmaker had already set the appointment; money had exchanged hands.

Ah-Ma saw the man she would marry the same day she was told of her fate. Unobserved by him, she peered out from behind the stairs of their flat to get a glimpse of him. My mother said she had no choice in the matter and thought he was ugly because his upper lip was split.

When I asked her why she married him, Ah-Ma said it was what her family decided. Since she had no other value, she would be the sacrificial lamb.

"What did you talk about when you first met him?" I asked.

Ah-Ma said, "Nothing."

Her marriage was a business transaction, she said. He got a wife, and Ah-Ma got to go to America. When Ah-Ma received her green card and later her citizenship, she was able to help her parents and siblings emigrate. She did it to give her siblings the hope of a better future.

Ah-Ma usually started crying at this point in the story, "Your father is a liar. He told me he came from a wealthy family. But I arrived in America and found out he doesn't have a penny and lived with his mother and father and six other people. He worked as a busboy! Kam Lee tricked me! He's good for nothing! And it was too late because I was already in America. Look, your father left you and your sister. He doesn't care about you. You think I wanted this life? No. I could've given you away to the orphanage. But I still took care of you. So, make sure you're not like Kam Lee. Are you going to leave me too when you grow up?"

"Never, Ah-Ma. I'll never leave you." These are the words that formed the boundaries of what it meant to be Bonnie Lee.

* * *

I was excited and nervous waiting for the elevator doors to open when I arrived that morning.

Portsmouth Square. This park, with more concrete than grass, sits on a sloping hillside, right above the parking lot I drove into earlier that morning. It's one of the few open spaces in Chinatown. It's everyone's front porch, earning the nickname of Chinatown's "living room."

It's been remodeled. I remember a tree here and there. They're gone.

One thing hasn't changed. The children are still tearing through the playground like metal balls ricocheting in a pinball machine. I stopped to look at the small children playing, who were the same age I would've been growing up there.

There's a lot of history here. Portsmouth Square is where the first American flag was raised in San Francisco, and in 1848, it was here that the discovery of gold was first announced. That sparked the Gold Rush, bringing immigrants from all over the world—including the Chinese who called San Francisco "Gold Mountain" (*Gum San*)—to build a better life for their families back home.

But while people from other nations were given access to citizenship, Chinese people were denied immigration in 1882 by the Chinese Exclusionary Act. The ban stood for nearly a century until the Civil Rights Amendment was signed in 1965. During this era, Chinese Americans were stripped of citizenship, the right to vote, the right to own property, and were barred entry to healthcare and hospitals outside of Chinatown.

That's why the Chinese Hospital that I was born in was created. It was the only way Chinese Americans received medical care. Chinese Americans were forced to stay in their box.

Sometimes, our life choices are just about survival. We make do with what's available to us, and we stay in our box.

Everything is safe. Familiar. There are no risks. You walk the same streets, say the same things, do the same things because you don't want to be alone. But, over time, the box becomes all you know.

Life is meant to be more than survival. There comes a time to step into a new world, beyond the box others have constructed for you. There comes a time you must leave the safety of what you know in order to embark on a new journey filled with risk. You do this in order to create a new life—a life of beauty and meaning.

Such a time came for me when I reached a crossroads at age 17, just like my mother had. I didn't know I was living in a box. I just thought that was my life…until someone showed me a life outside of the boundaries set for me. Until someone told me I needed to leave the world where Ah-Ma was my home and I was hers.

Remember my favorite wonton noodle shop sitting on Kearny Street bordering Chinatown in the east? Well, on the opposite side, on the outer limits of where Chinese Americans were told they could go or stay, you'll find the street that forms the western border of Chinatown: Powell Street. Powell is also the cross street where my childhood home is located. I was born and lived on the edge between two worlds. Not truly belonging to either.

At 17, I would make one of the most important decisions of my life. Would I choose to step out of the box? Or would I stay within the borders of the life that brought Ah-Ma to Chinatown? Would I venture forward without Ah-Ma's hand in mine?

> It is for freedom that Christ has set us free. Stand firm, then, and do not let yourselves be burdened again by a yoke of slavery (Galatians 5:1).

 ## LETTER TO MY YOUNGER SELF
You Are Worthy to Be Free

Beloved,

God has a plan for you, and it is also shaped by your decisions. You are free to change your mind and change course. You are free to be guided by God's love instead of by guilt and fear. You are free to be led by faith instead of by fate.

Following God's plan will require you to break out of the boxes, out of the roles others made for you. But happiness doesn't come from a life mapped out in certainty. Happiness comes from stepping into uncertainty, free to go where God guides you, with your hand lovingly held in His.

CHINESE FOLDING FANS

Chinese folding fans were invented 3,000 years ago—not for the function of cooling down, but as an art form. The paper and silk were a canvas. Men's fans were covered with stories written in calligraphy, reflecting their scholarly status. Women's were adorned with painted flowers and birds, symbolizing beauty and grace. Fans made of paper or silk were folded around ribs of sandalwood, ebony, tortoiseshell, ivory, mother of pearl, and bamboo.[1]

Like a beautiful fan, each chapter of our lives, through different seasons, tells a story and conveys a message meaningful for us. We weren't created merely to fulfill a functional need. We were created to reflect beauty as an original work of art by God.

Reflect and Share

- *What would you tell your younger self about fate?*

- *What are some of the boundaries, roles, or expectations that have been put on you? That you've taken on yourself? How is God inviting you to step out of those boxes?*

- *What are the boxes that society, family, friends, or the culture has defined for you? What are the cookie-cutter molds that are easy for you to fall into?*

Chapter 10

College

Located in the heart of Chinatown, there's something unusual that seems out of place in Portsmouth Square. At the edge of the park where old people play chess, across from the jungle gym where kids play, and next to the elevator for the underground garage, you'll find the Robert Louis Stevenson Memorial. It commemorates the Scottish author who lived a year near Chinatown in 1879, while writing essays, poetry, and fiction, eventually penning *Treasure Island*.

The inscription on the bronze memorial reads,

> To be honest, to be kind…
> to make upon the whole a family happier…
> above all…to keep friends with himself…
> Here is a task for all that man has of fortitude and delicacy.

I grew up giving my all to make my whole family happier. But to keep friends with myself? That was alien language; the concept did not fit in with my life. But one thing I knew: I did not want to end up in the same fate as Ah-Ma. I wanted to be like all my other school friends who wore rainbow Esprit sweatshirts and Guess jeans. I wanted to have a normal life where Ah-Ma didn't have to work temporary odd jobs in a factory for mere dollars, hunched over an assembly line plugging in electronic components onto a circuit board, meticulously hand-soldering components.

I was the one who would scour the newspaper and circle want ads for positions that didn't require a high school diploma. I called the numbers to apply for the positions, filled out the applications, and showed up to the interviews with my mother as her translator.

Looking back, it's pretty funny imagining what I sounded like as a little girl asking for a job on the phone, stating I was 28 years old and applying for a job, using my mom's name. I wonder what was running through the interviewers' minds as ten-year-old me sat across the desk from the men—the supervisors were always men—confessing at the reveal that I was the one calling for Ah-Ma all along because my mother couldn't speak English.

I know God used me to help my family in this way because we would eventually find a job. No matter how many interviews it took, I never gave up. For every "no" I received, I believed God would touch someone's heart to say "yes." God, bless those sweet souls who gave my mom a job!

I knew from doing all those interviews how important it was to get a high school diploma, but it never occurred to me that I could get a college degree. I wanted to have a better life for Ah-Ma and my little sister, who was five years younger than me, just a baby when my father left.

I dreamed of living in a house where I could invite friends over, where furniture matched, plastic dining chairs weren't duct taped, pipes didn't leak, the walls weren't grimy, the kitchen cabinets weren't chipped, and something wasn't always broken. I wanted to get Ah-Ma and my little sister out of the neighborhood where there was gang activity and drugs sold, where guys in low-riders carrying blasting boom boxes would catcall me on my walk home from school and ask whether I wanted to have a good time.

I was a straight-A student, but that didn't mean I wasn't mischievous. One day, I skipped school by calling in sick. (In addition to interpreting for Ah-Ma during interviews, I also pretended to be her in all things school related.) Since Ah-Ma was out working, I brought a friend over. I was cooking one of my precious packets of ramen noodles for us, usually saved for a special after-school snack, when she blurted, "Doesn't your mom ever clean the kitchen? There's grease everywhere!" She said it with a giggle to camouflage sounding aghast, but she never did come back.

Supposedly, everyone knows college is where the educated go. But how do you go to college if no one in your family asks you about it, if no one in your family has even graduated from high school or asks you about school because they're busy working, putting food on the table? Plus, how do you even think about the word *college* if you hardly have enough money to cover the rent, if fresh fruit is a luxury, and you only have one pair of shoes to last you until the soles start peeling?

You don't. The word *college* is just not part of your vocabulary. It's out of reach, like a thousand other outlandish things normal kids do, like going to Disneyland in the summer, having more than one pair of jeans in your drawer, or using a washing machine and dryer in your house instead of feeding quarters at the laundromat. I spent Saturday afternoons sitting on orange melamine chairs watching our clothes tumble in industrial sized-dryers because if I left, our clothes would most definitely get swiped.

If no one in your family talks about college or asks you about it, you just don't think about it. You just don't consider it an option. When you don't have money, you're disqualified from dreaming. So, I figured that after high school, I would get a job to help Ah-Ma with money. I didn't want to live month to month, but a high school diploma was the farthest I could see. It would be a great accomplishment from where I stood.

Don't ask for too much. Stay in your lane. Don't dream past what's practical.

The priority was taking care of my family. As for what happened to me personally, I would figure it out later as I went along, just as I always had.

But that wasn't what God had in mind for me. When we don't see a path ahead and settle for what we know, God sees a better way. God *makes* a way. God is not unfamiliar with our obstacles, and He starts from where we are.

God wanted me to ask for more in life. So, He sent me someone to help me ask questions I didn't know existed. Someone I didn't expect.

Mr. O'Neal was the first Black American I met in real life and interacted with personally. He ran a nonprofit summer job program at a computer lab at Foothill College for kids from low-income families, training youth on school-to-work transition skills. He was a tower of a man, standing over six feet tall. He wore khakis, dark brown leather loafers that matched his belt, buttoned-up plaid shirts, tortoiseshell glasses, and a pair of charming dimples. His diction made him sound like Mr. Huxtable.

He welcomed us on my first day on my first job—a ragtag group of Latino, Filipino, white, black, and Asian Americans—by writing his name, *Verley*, on the board. His name reminded me of what Jesus said often in the King James Bible: verily. Mr. O'Neal explained he would always be fair, but tough. He said he would always tell us the truth, and if we followed the rules of the program, we'd all get along just fine. He also introduced himself as the dean of the Computer Information Science department at the college. He told us he had graduated from Princeton.

Wow. An Ivy League school? I felt I was in the presence of royalty.

When we signed up for job slots, I was lucky enough to snag the computer lab assistant position, avoiding the maintenance jobs. One day, as I was formatting floppy discs, he asked me about college.

"Not sure," I replied. "I need to get a job after high school and take care of my mom and sister."

"What? No, you're not." Mr. O'Neal shot me a look that said, *Are you crazy? I don't think so.* "You are going to college, Miss Bonnie." Mr. O'Neal sat like a gentle giant at his desk. "I want you applying for Ivy League schools."

"You don't understand. I can't leave my mom." I didn't want to get into the details.

"Yes, you can. Your momma will be fine," Mr. O'Neal suddenly spoke plainly to me. Fatherly, firm, and yet kind. "You have a bright future. Don't stay. You gotta leave, girl."

I hadn't breathed a word about Ah-Ma or the way she was, nor the promise I'd made never to leave her. So I don't know how Mr. O'Neal knew, but I felt like he had stepped into my private home life.

"I can't afford it anyways," I replied, like a robot spitting out lines it's programmed to speak.

Mr. O'Neal turned in his swivel chair to face me. He looked dead serious. "You know you can get scholarships, don't you? Loans, interest free. What's your GPA, Bonnie?"

This conversation changed the trajectory of my life. I'd never heard of scholarships. I did not know the man I called my boss would become my mentor over four summers, guiding me on the path to higher education.

God always helped provide for my family, guiding the men who interviewed my mother to say yes. I always grew up believing that in matters of getting the rent paid, God miraculously provided the yeses. But would God give me a yes for myself? Would God change Ah-Ma's heart so she would let me go east and attend an Ivy League university?

Something I had never held in my heart ignited: hope.

God, will You answer this prayer for me? Will You get Ah-Ma to let me go?

Even though I had seen miracle upon miracle in the manna God provided for my family throughout the years, I was afraid. This hope was only fragile tinder. Could it grow into a steady flame? Or would it be snuffed out, leaving my heart darker for having once hoped in the wilderness?

No matter how many words Mr. O'Neal spoke into my life, I did not forget that I'd made a promise to Ah-Ma never to leave her. And I knew that Ah-Ma would not forget either.

> Hope does not disappoint, because the love of God has been poured out in our hearts by the Holy Spirit who was given to us (Romans 5:5 NKJV).

LETTER TO MY YOUNGER SELF
You Are Worthy of Hope

Beloved,

I know *hope* sounds like a foreign word to your soul. You think you can live without too much of it and soldier on. But living without hope is lonely.

Optimism is seeing how circumstances will get better, but hope is seeing God's love and care in the midst of bad circumstances. Hope is the refuge in uncertainty when optimism runs dry. To hope again is to believe God will help you.

Hope gives you permission to do things differently and to believe God will be faithful. Hope comes alive when you believe you are worthy of being loved. And Jesus loves you so much.

It might seem easier to just stay in survival mode and to simply maintain life, but God can renew your hope. Hope is the oxygen your soul breathes. It's never too late to have hope again.

CHINESE CHESS

Chinese chess (象棋) is called *zoeng kai* in Cantonese, meaning "elephant chess." This two-person board game dates to the first century, and it's played like Western chess. It's a game I watched old men play at the park—a battle between two armies of 16 pieces each, with the goal of capturing the king. In the middle of the board, dividing the two opposing sides, is the "river" which the elephant pieces cannot cross, while the soldier pieces gain advanced moves after crossing. Because the elephants can't move past the river, they can be easily trapped. But two elephants can defend each other.

In the same way, when we are isolated, we can feel trapped, unable to move. But when we come alongside each other to share our knowledge and support, we become strong and free to move across the board of life, freeing each other to move into new spaces.

Reflect and Share

- *What would you tell your younger self about hope?*

- *Ask yourself, "How can I live now, in a hopeful way?" instead of staying in survival mode, the status quo. How is God inviting you to hope again?*

- *Who is someone in your life that gave you hope?*

Chapter 11

My Mother's Daughter

On my first birthday after I earned my first paycheck, I wasn't making plans for a birthday party. Let's just say it wasn't part of our family culture. Instead, I grew up hearing my mother's admonition about what birthdays truly were for.

"You should be giving *me* a gift for giving you birth," Ah-Ma once told me when I asked her what it was like when I was born. "I was all alone, pregnant in America, no one to help me. I had to carry you for *nine months*—so sick, throwing up around the clock. I ended up lying in a hospital with a saline drip stuck in my arm." Ah-Ma explained the act of birthing me was her birthday gift to me each year.

"I'm sorry, Ah-Ma," I replied, fumbling to carry on the conversation. "What time was I born?" I asked, hoping to get to the good part.

"You couldn't come during the daytime. Nope. Smack in the middle of the night, you came out crying, screaming. Never stopped crying. Around the clock, that's all you did."

I apologized again, and Ah-Ma kept going. "Other people have babies they put down and go to sleep. Not you. I had to suffer, sitting up all night holding you, while I was bleeding down there, because your father's mother, Lai-Lai, would yell, 'What's wrong with you? Shut that crying baby up! You're keeping everyone awake!'"

According to my mother, I was least favored by my paternal grandmother because I wasn't a boy, and the family already had plenty of granddaughters. Ah-Ma once told me she chose to dress me in boys' clothes when I was little because she always wanted a boy instead of a girl, explaining why I'm not wearing dresses in any of my childhood photos, though she later denied ever saying so. Ah-Ma said, "Boys are better. They shoulder responsibilities. Can take care of the family. Girls? They grow up, marry into their husband's families, and they're gone."

This was not a story I could share in my new mothers' group when I later became pregnant with my first baby. The women asked each other, "What was it like when your mom gave birth?" to predict how difficult our birth experiences would be.

"My mom had morning sickness the whole time. It was a tough childbirth," was all I could say.

The women sighed empathetically, cheering me on, "You'll be okay. Your mom did it. You'll get through it too!"

I always felt so guilty for the burden I put my mom through. I really wanted to be a bright light in her life. So the day I ripped open the security envelope with a plastic window addressed to my name to pull out my first bona fide paycheck, I made sure to help my family. I gave Ah-Ma more money than what I tithed to God (with gratitude) and tucked away the rest in my bank account. I did not buy anything for myself. I saved it for college.

That winter for my birthday, I was so excited to make one withdrawal. I bought a pair of real leather, tan oxford flats, which were all the rage back in the '80s. I took out the crumpled balls of packing paper in each shoe and stuffed the toes of the flats with ten-dollar bills totaling $100. A world of money because it covered half our rent.

I wrapped the shoebox and hid it under my clothes in a drawer. On my birthday after dinner, I handed Ah-Ma my gift.

"Surprise!" I exclaimed. I could hardly contain my excitement. I felt so proud to finally give my mother something of worth, to make up for all the suffering she went through for me.

Ah-Ma opened the box, took out the paper bills, inspected the shoes, and turned to me. "Why did you crumple the bills? And these shoes. Did you buy them for me, hoping to borrow them for yourself?"

• • •

I wanted so badly to be a good daughter. Yet, I couldn't forget what Mr. O'Neal had said to me about college. Even if I did go away, I would still stay loyal to Ah-Ma. College could only help me to help our family.

This line of reasoning formed the basis of my escape plan. Behind the scenes, I spent hours with my high school career counselor to figure out the loans and grants, collecting college brochures and talking to college recruiters.

I set my sights on Ivy League schools. I wanted to live my life in a world inhabited by words and story—created by journalists, authors, poets, musicians, and literary professors.

Looking back at that 17-year-old me, I wish she hadn't told her momma her plans. I wish she had simply purchased a ticket, packed her bags, and flown east. But it didn't feel honest to mail out college applications without telling Ah-Ma. I decided on my opening arguments. *It won't cost any money. College will help me to help our family.* I waited to talk to her after I did the dishes after dinner.

She was in the living room watching TV when I sat beside her and asked if I could talk with her. "Ah-Ma, I'm gonna apply for college. I might go to the East Coast," I began, opening up college brochures, showing her how beautiful the campuses were.

Ah-Ma sat stone silent on our couch.

"I'm really good, Ah-Ma," I proceeded, just like I'd rehearsed it. "My English teachers all say I'm really good. And Mr. O'Neal says I can get in."

"Of course they'll say you're good." Ah-Ma's face grew ashen. "What do you expect? Mr. O'Neal runs that program for poor kids. Your teachers? They're Americans. They'll say you can do anything. But just because you think you're smart and speak English doesn't mean you're like them. You're Chinese."

Like an animal snared in a coil-spring trap, I was emptied of words.

I couldn't hear the voices of my teachers, Mr. O'Neal, or anyone else. The world filled with books and beautiful stories suddenly felt stupid and unreal.

"I've talked to the college recruiters. It's really hard to get in, but they say I've got a good chance," I countered. But, suddenly, I didn't feel so sure anymore.

Ah-Ma started shaking her head. "Those schools are for rich kids, families who have money. Not you."

Between scholarships, loans, financial aid, and money from summer and part-time jobs, I explained how I had worked out covering the cost. But instead of helping my case, my plans added fuel to the fire, infuriating Ah-Ma.

"If you go, who will take care of me? And your sister?" She was getting angrier by the minute. "You… a writer… a journalist? I know you. *You're just selfish.* You just want to travel the world and leave me. You weren't so high and mighty when you were small and needy. Now you have wings, you want to fly away and have the good life?"

Her words slayed me with a thousand cuts. I broke down sobbing, begging her to stop.

"You've forgotten who you are. You are Bonnie Lee. *You are my daughter.*" She stood up now, gathering strength over me.

"If you leave, you're on your own." My mother drew a line in the sand. "I'll move away, take your sister with me, and you'll never see us again. You'll come back to an empty house." Because I paid our bills and knew we rented month to month, I knew she could make good on her threat.

"Don't ever call me Ah-Ma again." Her words cursed the air. "Have your happy life. But I won't be a part of it. And you'll be pitiful. Because everyone will have family, except you. You'll have nothing."

Ah-Ma left me trailing behind her as she marched back to her bedroom and slammed the door in front of me. The brochures in my hands felt wrong—no longer shiny, glossy, and new. This other beautiful life was not possible for me.

As I stood there blinded by tears, I saw my little sister lying on the bed across the hallway and wrapped in covers, hiding from the battle that had ensued.

It's too late for me, I thought. *But it's not too late for her. I can make money. Take care of my mother and give my sister the chance to choose her future when it's time for her to leave.*

And that's how I walked through the same doorway of fate Ah-Ma walked through when she was 17, when she chose to marry a stranger ten years older to give her siblings a better future. That was the moment I chose to step into my mother's world. I was, after all, my mother's daughter, and that was not something I could change. I had thought I could live in both the world with Ah-Ma and the world of who I wanted to become. But I was wrong.

I decided to stay nearby. I chose to enroll at UCLA to become a computer engineer. I turned around, walked into the kitchen, and shoved my college brochures down—past the empty milk carton, leftover dinner scraps, and junk mail—into the garbage can.

•••

We can't live in two worlds. Sooner or later, we all have to face the moment where we must choose who we want to be. Each of us has the freedom to choose where we want to live: in the world someone carved for us or in the world we created on our very own.

Now that I had made my choice, I fully embraced my Chinese identity. My mother was right. I was her daughter. That wasn't something I could change.

After all, I had prayed for years in anticipation of this moment, asking God to help me to get a yes from Ah-Ma to let me go east to college. If God could change Pharaoh's heart to let His people go and nothing was impossible for Him, surely He would have made it happen for me if He wanted it, I reasoned. I guessed God's answer to me was a no because Ah-Ma's answer was no.

So, I accepted by faith that this must all have been God's plan. Maybe all these dreams I carried weren't meant to be lived in my life on earth, I surmised.

This was the moment I lost my voice. I believed life was made easier and the blade of pain more blunted this way. I didn't know that God was still at work protecting the seeds of hope of who I was created to be, and that my story was still being written. I couldn't see the measures God was putting in place to restore the years the locusts were eating away. I didn't understand God was making a way for the impossible.

I steeled my heart, resigned to walking my path with my heart disconnected and cocooned. Lonely and unseen. I learned this truth at 17.

> The threshing floors shall be full of wheat, and the vats shall overflow with new wine and oil. So I will restore to you the years that the swarming locust has eaten (Joel 2:24-25 NKJV).

 ## LETTER TO MY YOUNGER SELF
You Are Worthy to Have Dreams

Beloved,

God will restore to you the years the locusts have eaten.

Don't give up. The dreams you once tried to forget are remembered by your loving Savior. He saw your heart break as your dreams shattered into thousands of pieces.

You are not forgotten. Jesus is collecting all your tears in a bottle, recording every moment in His journal. He does this to let you know that behind every dream lost lies the greater dream of Him loving you more intimately and deeply, so that one day, you will dare to dream again.

Don't be afraid. You are good soil. The dreams God planted in your heart will later blossom, watered with the tears you shed today. God will make beautiful things grow again.

THE ANCIENT ART OF WEAVING

Among ancient China's greatest inventions, silk weaving lands at the top of the list. China was the first civilization to use silk. According to legend, silk cloth was first invented 4,000 years ago by Lei Zu, the wife of the Yellow Emperor, when she was having tea in the garden and a silk cocoon fell into her tea and unraveled. She discovered that the thread was long, strong, and soft. She combined the silk fibers into a thread and invented the silk loom that turned the threads into a luxurious cloth.

When we go through hard times that sideline us in life, God, the Master Weaver, uses all the details to create beautiful patterns in the fabric of our life. As Joseph told his brothers in Genesis 50:20, "You intended to harm me, but God intended it for good." The root word in Hebrew for *intended* means "to weave." God is an artist, and He is at work weaving goodness into every chapter of your life.

Reflect and Share

- *What would you tell your younger self about her dreams?*

- *What dreams is God inviting you to explore or breathe new life into?*

- *What were your dreams in an earlier part of your life? What inspired you to pursue them, or what hindered them?*

Chapter 12

Homeland

When I was a little girl growing up in Chinatown in the '70s, there were no TV cable channels, VHS tapes, or DVDs to watch movies. If you wanted to catch the latest flick, you did what anyone did back then: You checked the daily papers for show listings, and you headed to the theaters.

For first generation Chinese Americans like my mother and father, Chinese movies were one of the few diversions available to take a break from the drudgery of working brutal restaurant hours six days a week. They missed Hong Kong, and they could feel connected by watching movies from their homeland.

Ah-Ma didn't have many friends. Her only escape was taking me every day to watch back-to-back matinee shows. The movies she took me to watch were all made during Hong Kong Cinema and Taiwan's Golden Age and were played in theaters that exclusively showed Chinese-speaking films. The Great Star Theatre, built in 1925, and Grandview Theatre, built in 1940, were located on the same street as the hospital and my childhood home!

Although I lived in America, the only world I saw was Hong Kong, where Ah-Ma came from. What people ate, where they went to school, the open-air street restaurants they ate at (*dai pai dong*), the uniforms they wore walking to school, and the shops tucked into the concrete high-rise neighborhoods all became a part of my neural network of the sights and sounds of childhood. The first conversations from which I observed how people loved and hated, of friendship, romance, and family—what they cried over, laughed about, fought over, dreamed, and aspired to attain—all played out in the stories of people back "home" in Hong Kong and Taiwan.

As a result, I grew up downloading life in Hong Kong virtually, living vicariously through the songs and pop culture I drank in, sitting in the dark, watching films flash on the big screen. Sam Hui, along with his brothers Michael and Ricky, cracked me up. They are comedic versions of the Marx Brothers and Peter Sellers—lovable misfits acting out visual gags in Cantonese slang. I laughed watching classics like *The Private Eyes* and *Chicken and Duck Talk*.

Now, what might shock you is that one of my favorite types of movie as a little girl wasn't just comedy or romance. Once a week, when my father had a day off work, he took me to theaters, where we spent hours watching Shaw Brothers Kung Fu movies, always in double features (you'd be foolish not to get your money's worth).

So, while my future husband, Eric, was watching *Star Wars: Episode IV: A New Hope* in 1978, little me was standing in line to watch the premiere of Jackie Chan's *Drunken Master*. And, of course, I was a fan of Bruce Lee, since we were born in the same hospital in Chinatown!

I always wanted to visit the country where all these movies were made. So, I decided I ought to see Hong Kong and China for myself before heading off to college.

With part of my savings, I bought two tickets to travel to Hong Kong and China. One for Ah-Ma and one for me. It was the first time my mother would return to Hong Kong since she was 17.

The village within Guangdong where my grandparents came from is called the Xinwui district. I wanted to see the place where my grandparents, Ah-Ma, and her siblings had escaped from the Communists during the 1950s. They'd crossed over to British Hong Kong as refugees before the Bamboo Curtain fell during the Cultural Revolution, and

Mao Tse Tung closed the borders. Families with members still left in China were split apart and separated. It was a historical turning point in China's history. Millions of people like my grandparents escaped to the island of Hong Kong, while other people retreated to begin an independent government on the island of Taiwan.

My maternal great-grandfather, who was 90 years old, was still living in the village in Guangdong when I arrived. He, along with my grandmother Po-Po's brothers and sisters (my great-uncles and great-aunts), never made it out. We telephoned them long distance to ask if someone could meet us at the train station.

I didn't know what to expect because there were never any photos of Ah-Ma or my grandparents when they lived in China. There was no Internet back then, so it's not like I could Google what the village looked like. I naively guessed it looked like the China shown on PBS documentaries, portrayed in two colors—either urban cities or beautiful countryside rice paddies. I imagined it looked like the folksy natural landscapes I had seen in the brush paintings displayed in the stores of Chinatown.

But when I arrived in my great-grandfather's home, the single room I sat in was not like any of those images. The walls were crumbled and broken in many spots. The doorframe was chipped, sunken down, not plumb. Water-leak spots left their rings on the ceiling. A constant stream of people came to the door—friends and neighbors cheerfully poking their heads in, full of wide smiles and waving hello. I must have been introduced I don't know how many times. My cheeks were hurting from all the smiling, but I felt ecstatic and honored to be such a welcomed guest.

When they introduced me to the extended family around the table—I couldn't keep track of the who's-who of cousins, aunts, in-laws, wives, husbands, nephews, nieces, and friends—they didn't call me Bonnie.

"This is *Sook-Wah!*" For the first time, someone called me by my real Chinese name. I instantly felt 100 percent Chinese. "She's Law Cheung's granddaughter! Visiting from America!" they exclaimed, while encircling a loving arm around mine. Law Cheung was the name of my Po-Po, and this was her village and family.

There was so much food coming out of the kitchen. The whole table was completely full of every possible form of meat—chicken, pork, beef, fish; steamed, stir-fried, braised—and there were mushrooms, lots of green vegetables, and bone-broth soup, and for dessert, there was fruit. I couldn't help but feel completely indebted to them for pulling out all the stops. It was apparent they were going above and beyond, splurging to host me.

I kicked myself for not buying more presents to take with me from America. I didn't bring enough for everyone. I thought I was only meeting my grandma's brother and sister, their spouses, and my great-grandfather. They asked a thousand questions, and I could hardly eat between answers, although hands with chopsticks kept reaching out across the table to put food in my bowl, telling me to "Eat more! Eat more!"

I was the first American they had met, and they could not ask me enough questions about what life was like in the *Mei-Guo*—the "beautiful country" of America. I felt like a talk show host, asking questions in return about their lives, hearing some of the most amazing stories.

They gave me the place of honor, seated next to my great-grandfather, whom I called Baak-Gung. I was constantly pouring him tea, asking if I could serve him more mushrooms, and offering him the best piece of chicken breast. I could not help but want to constantly hug him. He was so tiny, but spry and smiley. The amazing thing is that my Baak-Gung kept hugging me back, holding on to me the whole night too! Tears of joy were streaming down his face, and he was always wiping his eyes. He told everyone he thought I was very pretty and said I looked like a Hong Kong movie and pop star from the '80s, Sally Yeh. Baak-Gung was all smiles, asking me if I liked to sing.

"I love to sing!" I replied. "Would you like me to sing you a song?"

My great-aunt heard the conversation and said, "Everybody quiet! Sook-Wah is going to sing us all a song!"

So I sang a song in Chinese about God's love. I sang about how God is our Heavenly Father, and He cares for us like the wildflowers and the birds of the air. My heart blossomed to share the gospel by sharing that song. Everyone listened politely and exploded with applause when I finished. I offered a few words to explain the song and to share that I was a Christian.

My great-uncle, sitting across from me, looked suddenly despondent. "Well, I'm glad you're living such a happy life in America," he said. "But you don't know the suffering we are living."

My great-aunt shot him a look and said, "Don't talk about such things. We're eating." But my great-uncle was not assuaged. He told me how my great-grandfather had suffered during the Cultural Revolution, was imprisoned for years, losing all his property and possessions. He continued recounting at length a story of how the family was struggling, beginning to cry as he spoke about his bitterness and sorrows. I had never seen an elderly Chinese man weep before, and my heart broke apart too.

At this point, my great-uncle's son—my grandmother's nephew—stepped over to put his hand on his father's shoulder and told him, "Okay, okay. That's good for now. They just got here. We can talk more later."

But my great-uncle did not agree. "No. Sook-Wah needs to know the truth. She's the only one to make the effort to come back, and that means she cares. She is family. Right, Sook-Wah?" he asked me. I nodded.

Many people got up from the table at this point and began to clear the dishes, but my great-uncle was getting down to brass tacks. He had a plea.

"Sook-Wah, this God you speak of must have a plan for our family by bringing you back to us. You can be God's way to help us emigrate to America. You are young. You can marry my son."

I couldn't believe what he was saying.

"Now, I know you don't have affection for each other. So, after a few years, after rescuing our family to America, you can always separate. It wouldn't cost you anything. No hard feelings. By doing this, you will be our family's rescuer *gao-yan-yun*. What do you think?"

I look over at Ah-Ma. She didn't say a thing.

"I know you've had to suffer so much," I replied with a frog in my throat. "But I haven't even *thought* of marriage." I was embarrassed to say I was going to college when everybody in the room was struggling in poverty.

My great-aunt broke the silence, "Okay, that's enough for now. Let's get the oranges. Everybody, let's eat some fruit!"

• • •

Later that night, back at the hotel, as we lay in darkness on our beds, I asked Ah-Ma why she hadn't stood up and spoken for me.

"There's no use saying anything to Great Uncle," Ah-Ma said matter-of-factly. "It's obvious he planned that speech. Let him talk. It's harmless."

I guess so. I am leaving in a few days. I put it out of my mind and turned over to sleep.

The next day, the family made plans to take us sightseeing. They took us to some old ruins outside the city. "It's a great place to take pictures," they told us.

The whole family was going—an entourage of people. Some of the women and girls walked with me, each of them giving me token gifts to take home to the U.S. The gifts they gave me weren't new, but I knew they were treasured possessions, like a little wooden keychain with a bell. Another girl gave me a puffy, embroidered satin fish. One relative gave me a floral pad of paper the size of a small Post-it note, while another handed me a pencil and eraser with a cat stamped in its design. I graciously thanked them many times over and hugged them in return.

As we arrived at a picturesque park dotted with stone memorials, Great Uncle's son asked to show me something he thought I would like very much over at another part of the park. I followed him, but as we walked over, I got a distinct feeling I was walking into a conversation I did not want to have with this young man.

I told him I was going to college in the fall.

He replied that he was happy for me, and while he wished he could go to college, he had humble goals in life. He just wanted to help provide for his family—would I understand that?

"Of course," I replied.

My mind was racing in a thousand directions because I guessed where this conversation was heading. I did not want to find myself in a position where I had to reject this man's plea to help the family.

Bonnie, preserve his dignity. Leave now.

"Great Uncle's son," I began, "thank you for bringing me here. I know you have so many dreams and desires to take care of your family. It's hard for me too. Ah-Ma expects me to fulfill so many of her dreams. But you know, even though I can speak and understand Chinese, I'm really an American. I'm caught between two worlds myself. So, I'm still finding my way."

He was surprised by my words, and I believe we had an honest, unspoken understanding because Great Uncle's son smiled and said, "I understand. I understand." Then, he spoke in broken English, "I wish…you best."

* * *

That is the moment I caught a glimpse of what it means to come home to who I really was. Honoring your no is more important than saying yes and losing yourself. It happened when I was far, far away, thousands of miles from my own homeland: *America.*

For the first time, I learned that although I deeply longed to honor my family, I was able to say no and honor my heart. I was grateful my cousin once removed was so very gracious, and I'll always remember how respectfully he handled the conversation.

There were still many more miles for me to travel on this journey of finding pieces of who God created me to be as a woman of worth, and the life I wanted to lead as Bonnie Sook-Wah Lee. But this was a beginning.

Let your "Yes" be "Yes," and your "No," "No"
(Matthew 5:37 NKJV).

LETTER TO MY YOUNGER SELF
Your No Is Worth Honoring

Beloved,

Your no is worth honoring.

You shouldn't have to change who you are to satisfy anyone. So let your yes be yes, and let your no be no.

You know how the world is. They will never be happy with just one compromise. Even if you try to please others and prioritize satisfying their needs above yours, their demands won't ever end. When you avoid honoring your no, you become more insecure, losing sight of your yes.

You can't tell your story or live your life honestly if you edit your heart—if you align with anyone else's values instead of your own. Be brave. Say no simply. Be honest about why. Say yes to God and not to people.

CHINESE COURTYARD SIHEYUAN

Siheyuan refers to classic Chinese architecture for a typical residence for the wealthy and successful: a courtyard surrounded by different buildings on each of its four sides, dating back through 2,000 years of history. The pattern of the home reveals the Chinese philosophy of what is considered a good life, and family is central. A red door signifies good fortune. A screen wall is placed inside the gate for privacy, so passersby cannot see into the house. The northern building has the most sunlight, and that prime spot is given to the grandparents, as heads of the family, and their living room is where the family gathers. On the east, the next most favored location is reserved for the oldest son and his wife. They hold the highest status, since the inheritance passes to them next. The building on the west is for the second son. Women are placed in the back, behind the main house, because women were not allowed to be easily seen by company.[1]

Each of us is like a home where the Holy Spirit lives. Each of us also has the freedom to establish boundaries, the freedom to design life in the unique way God inspires in each of us.

Reflect and Share

- *What would you tell your younger self about the value of saying no?*

- *What are the things God is inviting you to let go of or to say no to? What helps make it easier to say no, and what makes it difficult?*

- *When was a time in your life that saying no meant disappointing someone else?*

Chapter Thirteen

Lotus Flower

The souvenir shops in Chinatown set along Grant Avenue are fun to browse through. One shop especially captured my attention because to me it wasn't a store, but an art gallery.

This shop sold Chinese brush paintings. Beautiful Chinese mountain landscapes—depicting waterfalls, bamboo, and idyllic sampan boats dotting the river—covered the walls. But my favorite brush paintings were the big blossoms of flowers—chrysanthemum, peonies, or plum blossoms and lotus flowers—painted on paper scrolls hanging vertically like curtains of artwork.

One of the most beloved Chinese flowers is the lotus. Lotus flower roots are planted in mud, yet after every night of being submerged in river water, they miraculously blossom again with perfectly white petals the next morning. The lotus flower is special to the Chinese people because it is the symbol for purity and beauty.

Monet himself went crazy painting water lilies in 250 works of art, one famously titled *Lotus Flowers*. I understand Monet's passion to capture the lotus flower's splendor because there was a moment in my life I was like the lotus flower, trying to find beauty in the muddy waters of my life.

It happened in a place where I thought I was safe from harm, where my innocence would be protected. But life went off script.

• • •

I was a freshman at UCLA—an exciting time away from the prying eyes of Ah-Ma. The days of daydreaming about going on dates in high school were over, and I was eager to embark on my new dating life, just as the little girl in me had dreamed.

There weren't that many Chinese Americans in my high school. So, when I went to college, fresh from my visit to China, I decided to immerse myself into my Chinese roots. I signed up for the Chinese Student Association and the Hong Kong Student Association. I joined the Asian American Christian Fellowship and the Chinese Christian Fellowship campus ministries.

I carried a duo language Chinese-English Bible that showed Scripture in English in one column and Chinese in the other, so I could follow along as friends read in Chinese. My overseas-born Chinese (OBC) friends adopted me as their ABC sister (American-Born Chinese). I even attended the Baptist Church in Chinatown, which took an hour to reach in Friday night traffic in downtown Los Angeles.

It was during my year of Chinese immersion, listening to Cantonese pop music, doing Bible studies in Chinese, and attending worship in Chinese, that I went on my first date ever.

The first person who asked me out was a Chinese Christian guy—a foreign student from Hong Kong. (Let's call him The Guy, shall we?) We met in one of the Bible studies I attended. The Guy wore Ralph Lauren polo shirts and had nice hair like Tom Cruise, with a winning smile to match. He was a year older than me.

The Guy was soft-spoken and well-liked by everyone. We were entering spring quarter, so we had known each other most of the school year, having gone on ministry retreats, to social outings, and to countless meetings as a community. Because everyone was away from home, the Christian community felt like one big family.

So it was exciting when The Guy asked me out on a date, and I felt safe since he was known in my circle of Bible study leaders. Who knows, maybe I would find Prince Charming in college, right? He picked me up at my dorm. I was wearing a cute jean skirt with a new top I bought for the date.

"I need to stop by my house to pick up some mail to drop off at the post office," The Guy said after opening the car door for me. "That okay, before we head to lunch?"

Oh, cool. I get to see where he lives, I thought. I would get more clues into what this guy was like.

"Do you want to come in while I grab my mail?" he asked, pulling the car into the parking space.

Once inside, The Guy gave me a tour of the house, and I noticed how neat and new everything was. I was impressed. This guy was ticking off points left and right.

I sat on the living room couch, waiting for him, and then he returned to sit next to me and started chatting. He wrapped his arms around me. Before I knew what was happening, he kissed me.

I was surprised; I had imagined our first kiss wouldn't happen until we held hands. But here it was. The kiss was happening. I closed my eyes to see if this was going to be all I hoped a kiss would be.

But it didn't go the way a girl ought to be kissed by her date. The kiss turned into something more, and as I tried to push him away, he started overpowering me and pressed me down against the sofa. With my body pinned down, I couldn't kick him off.

I fought to wrangle myself off the couch cushions, but that only made things worse, because now we fell onto the ground where there was no give for me to fight him off and escape. I battled to get away, but he shoved me up against the side of the wall. I was trapped.

It was like a switch had flipped, and all I remember was total chaos of arms and legs flailing, shoving, kicking, each of us desperate to overpower the other. I screamed as I was sending a thunder of fists raining down on his head—"Stop it! Stop it! STOP!"—but to no avail. Every time I tried to fight him off, I was rendered defenseless. My screams disappeared into thin air while *it* happened.

I went into the shock of survival mode. I told myself it wasn't happening. *It's just my body,* I kept saying to myself.

After it was over, The Guy said nothing. I didn't want him to think I was afraid, because maybe he would hurt me more. I made my way to the bathroom, locked the door, looked in the mirror, and told myself, "You are okay. You are okay, Bonnie." But I wasn't.

On the ride back, The Guy acted like nothing had happened as music played from his CD deck. The only thing he said was, "I'll call you later." Then he dropped me off.

• • •

I went up to my dorm room and took a shower. I started shaking. My body began trembling uncontrollably, and I sobbed, the cascade of water my refuge.

Was God going to punish me? No good Christian guy will want me.

These were the words flooding my soul in the shower. I'd sat through years of purity talks in high school church, hearing how important it was to preserve my worth and my value. If I saved myself, one day I'd give myself as a gift to my husband.

Where does that leave me now? What do I have to offer anymore? As fear filled the pit of my stomach, one person came to my mind.

Emma. Emma was my high school girls' leader at church. Before I left for college, Emma told me I could call her anytime. She said she would always be there for me. I walked down to the dorm lobby, dropped some coins in the pay phone, punched in her number, and waited.

• • •

"Hello?"

When I heard Emma's voice, I broke down crying so hard that I couldn't talk for several minutes.

"What is it, Bonnie? Are you okay?" she kept asking, her voice stricken with concern. "What happened?" Every time Emma said something, I just started crying, choking over my tears all over again.

Emma finally said, "Bonnie, I want you to take a deep breath." She spoke with such gentleness, it calmed me. "Everything is going to be okay," she continued. "You are going to be okay. I'm here for you."

I began to tell her everything that happened. This was the beginning of a conversation that would change the direction of what it meant for me to be beloved. Emma did not start by quoting Scripture, asking me, "Why didn't you…" or lecturing, "You should have…" Her heart broke with mine as she relived the moment with me.

She asked me if I was safe and looked after my well-being the way a loving sister would. Emma said that nothing can ruin the value of God's love for me. She told me it wasn't my fault. She told me that whoever God had chosen for me as my future husband would love me and treasure me unconditionally.

At the time, I doubted it. But her reassuring words would echo in my heart like a touchstone throughout the years, when I wondered if I'd ever find anyone to love me.

"What do you think of me, now that this happened?" I asked.

What Emma said next helped safeguard my sense of worth, and I will never, ever forget the words spoken over the receiver that day. "I don't see you any less, Bonnie. You are still the beautiful girl I know and love. Nothing will ever change that. God will use this in your life." Her voice remained unwavering. "I know you'll continue to glorify God, just as you always have. God will use everything in your life to be a testimony. You are special. I know it."

Those were the beautiful words God set in my heart like a sparkling North Star, and I lovingly whisper this same message of *broken made beautiful* to you, friend, in whatever situation you find yourself. Because to be human is to be broken, and to be broken is to be made beautiful when you fall into the loving arms of Jesus, who cares for every wound you have sustained as His very own.

I cried, standing there at the pay phone in my sweats and flip-flops, but this time, my tears came from the relief of love and acceptance.

Emma's words and her story were a beacon of hope, a lighthouse calling ships home from sea.

● ● ●

My true worth isn't based on nothing "bad" happening to me. What affirms my true worth is that God sent someone to love me when I felt unlovable and ruined.

God can transform the bad that happens in this life and use it for good. We can use that power to comfort, lift, and give life to others who need hope. We can only do that as fellow sojourners, instead of people who preach but have never lived our humanity. Whatever tragedy has happened on your journey, God wants to transform it into healing power. We can tell someone, "You are safe with me. I'm here for you." We can say, "You are beautiful" and restore the dignity that Jesus gives through our voice. Love heals.

God sent Emma to stand with me in my moment of brokenness and transformed it into sisterhood. That moment was no longer marked only by shame. Instead, wrapped in the loving presence of someone who still believed in me, I found healing in the light.

The lotus flower is regarded as one of the most beautiful with its delicate petals blossoming in soft pink and pure white. But remember: What makes the lotus flower so special is that its roots are formed in muddy, murky river water, and yet it is undeterred, miraculously blooming brilliantly in harsh conditions, without residue on its petals.

You can do the same, my friend. You can be God's light. You are the lotus flower. You are rooted in love as God's beloved daughter. God wants to heal us, love us, and not shame us. Faith is the intimate act of trusting God with your real self instead of hiding how you feel.

Healing the heart that you've put to the side may be the most powerful act of faith that God is calling you to make today. Tell someone. And if the pain still lingers, find someone to help you investigate your story, a therapist to guide you through, and don't stop until you find the right one that works for you.

Healing from emotional abuse, whether verbal or physical, is the radical choice to be the beloved, a channel of God's redemption and hope. With this newfound peace, we become wounded healers. Everyone has a story. How beautiful is our gift of love and acceptance in this lonely world where everyone hides.

We are beautiful people rescued by grace, offering that rescue to others. We can say to each other, "You are beautiful. You are loved. You are going to be okay. You are worthy of healing. You are worthy to shine your light."

In time, as I healed, I learned to honor what the young woman in me went through. I won't push her away. She deserves to be nurtured and celebrated. I remind myself to be gentle with her. The woman in me is a flower learning to open up and blossom again.

> [People do not] light a lamp and put it under a bowl. Instead they put it on its stand, and it gives light to everyone in the house. In the same way, let your light shine (Matthew 5:15-16).

 ## LETTER TO MY YOUNGER SELF
You Are Worthy to Shine

Beloved,

My scars remind me that I'm not only a survivor; I am a warrior of God's grace. I am living proof that God's healing love is real. I am who I am today because I appreciate the kindness that was shown to me, and now I open my heart as a restful sanctuary to love those God sends me.

Jesus, give me courage to heal whenever there is more wholeness that Your love is freeing me to receive. Give me courage to shine Your light wherever Your power is empowering me to speak.

Thank You for taking care of me. I'm grateful for Your gentle touch to restore me. Thank You for loving me.

CHINESE LANTERNS:
BEAUTIFUL LIGHT

Your life is like a beautiful silhouette where light shines through a pattern, like the picture you see through the cutout on a Chinese lantern. During Chinese New Year, a time to usher in the return of spring and newness, Chinese people hang elaborate lanterns to decorate their streets and homes. The art of paper cutting was developed during the Han Dynasty in the fourth century AD after the Chinese official Cai Lun invented paper in AD 105. Craftsmen created paper-cutting art to decorate lanterns with intricate silhouettes. As light is emitted from the lantern, the beautiful designs shine through![1]

We are God's lantern. Each of us has stories—patterns shaped by our lives—that show a picture of how much God loves us when His light shines through. God takes the painful things and uses them to shine His radiant light in you. So, share God's love through the unique silhouette of your soul and story.

Reflect and Share

- *What would you say to your younger self about God's healing love?*

- *How has God transformed something bad into something good in your life?*

- *What was a moment in your life when God sent someone to be a light to you?*

  Picture them. What they said. What they did. Write a note, call, or text that person to express the light they have been for you. Think of them. Thank God for them. Ask God to bless them.

Chapter 14

Survivor's Guilt

Survivor's guilt. It's a feeling you carry, knowing you escaped a traumatic event when others did not. You carry a heavy responsibility with the freedom you secured.

It's how I felt going away to college, leaving Ah-Ma and my sister back home. When you work really hard to accomplish a goal with the responsibility to provide for others, you feel pressured to make opportunities count. You don't squander the chances you're given on something as impractical as personal fulfilment. My college years felt like maybe what a soldier feels when he has R&R leave between tours of active duty. You enjoy your time away, but in the back of your mind, the truth is lurking.

This reprieve is temporary. One day, you'll be called back into active duty, back onto the frontlines on the battlefield.

So, while my fellow collegiates were having the time of their lives, free to explore life away from home, I carried a hidden burden. Knowing I needed to account for my time away from Ah-Ma, I spent my college years hurrying to graduate, studying alongside electrical engineering majors, and burning all-nighters coding in UCLA's Boelter Hall—what we called *The Dungeon*.

The years passed by in a blur. College felt more like a long test of endurance to complete my engineering classes quickly. I needed to graduate and earn a paycheck so I could help Ah-Ma escape from our bad neighborhood and get my little sister launched to college.

The joy I found came from my passion for studying God's Word and serving people in ministry. I became very active in leading ministries and found a sense of belonging by serving in community. Once I graduated with my bachelor's degree in computer science and engineering, I followed the yellow brick road to wear khakis and a blazer and climb the corporate ladder in Silicon Valley. I enjoyed the intellectual challenge of working in the real world in high tech, as a woman in a male-dominated industry. But in my heart, I longed to find deeper meaning. I began asking God, *What is Your calling in my life?*

I attended missions conferences, went on a summer missions trip to Hong Kong, and began reading about life as a missionary. I kept returning to the question of whether God was calling me to serve in full-time overseas ministry.

Years before, after visiting our relatives in China, Ah-Ma and I had entered Hong Kong to play tourist in Causeway Bay, where my grandparents had settled to raise Ah-Ma and her seven siblings in the '50s after World War II when the Communist Party took power in the mainland. British Hong Kong was exciting—a vibrant, modern, and sophisticated city alive with so much energy, personality, amazing and delicious food, and shopping! Riding the subway there, I stood as tall as a giraffe, easily reaching the grab handles instead of precariously hanging on like I did back in the States. I moved freely among the citizens of Hong Kong, feeling at ease speaking the language, blending into the culture that I once observed in the theaters and while grocery shopping and making daily life with shopkeepers in Chinatown. I looked like everyone else in Hong Kong.

That seed of belonging germinated eight years later after graduation, when, after working four years in high tech, I felt called to serve as an overseas missionary in Hong Kong. I was 26 years old, attending a Christian conference, and leading a parachurch Chinese student ministry when a guest speaker from Hong Kong made a passionate call for Chinese American young adults to return in 1997. That's when British citizenship would be lost as the island returned back to China's rule. Privileged Hong Kongers, armed with wealth, education, and connections, were emigrating to Canada, the U.S., and Britain, leaving the colony en masse, while everyday working-class people could not.

"Remember your roots!" the charismatic speaker blared from the pulpit. "God must have a purpose for you who are citizens of America. Will you answer the call to serve? Like the prophet Isaiah replied, when God asked, 'Who will I send?' will you stand up and say, 'Send me!?'"

I stood up. *Yes!* This was the call I had been preparing to answer my whole life. Suddenly, my weirdly shaped life that never fit anywhere took on a higher purpose.

I don't fit in anywhere because it means I can be sent anywhere by God, to love and serve! I concluded. Everything made total sense, even the fact that the Bible I read from since childhood was bilingual. As I sat in church Sundays hearing the sermon given in Cantonese, I followed along in English. I had the best of both worlds to offer as I loved on the young people of Hong Kong. I felt I had found my identity in the apostle Paul's words, "I have become all things to all people so that by all possible means I might save some" (1 Corinthians 9:22).

God had given me so much during the formative years of my youth. It was time to give back. I stood up with tears streaming down my face, walking down the aisle to dedicate myself to serve in overseas missions.

I gave notice to my boss, Bruce, at work. My manager was concerned for my well-being and the uncertain political climate. "Let's set this up as a leave of absence," Bruce advised. "You don't know what will happen after the changeover."

I assured him my plans wouldn't change. I had signed a contract to serve as a missionary for five years, and missionary funds among supporters had been successfully raised beyond what I needed. I was positive of my one-way ticket.

I lugged my bed, living room sofa, dining table, desk, and the kitchen sink out of my duplex for a yard sale and sold everything I owned in one weekend. Including the first car I ever owned out of college: a green Acura Integra. I packed two suitcases, secured my passport and visas, had a big party with all my supporters who encircled me, laying hands on me to pray. We all bawled a Kleenex mess, as everyone joined hands to sing.

And Ah-Ma? She boarded the flight overseas, sitting next to me, because where would Ah-Ma go, if I left her in the States? We both checked in our baggage, like a husband taking his wife onto the mission field. We were mother and daughter forever.

• • •

Although everything felt familiar on my first visit to Hong Kong when I was a teen, one oddity surprised me. When we asked for the check after a meal, we'd get the bill, but there was no fortune cookie on the plastic tip tray. Weird, right?

I loved breaking open the cookies, pulling the strips of paper out, and having a good laugh, hearing everyone go around reading predictions like "A beautiful, smart, and loving person will be coming into your life" or "A lifetime of happiness lies ahead of you." Not to mention, the vanilla crunchy wafers are just yummy. They're a game and treat folded up in one.

Having grown up in the Bay Area, I always assumed fortune cookies were from China. I was wrong. Fortune cookies were invented in California, made en masse and popularized in San Francisco after World War II, as Chinese American restaurants tucked them in as a novelty, courtesy dessert. Americans loved them. In fact, there are approximately 3 billion fortune cookies made each year, most for the United States market.

I would soon learn that I was more like the American-made fortune cookie instead of accepted as authentic Chinese when I arrived for my first day on the job as a missionary. I was serving as a counselor with The Youth Ministry in Kowloon, taking at-risk, delinquent youth on Outward Bound nature camp experiences, which culminated in gospel camps to share the love of Jesus with them.

I am what Chinese people call ABC: American Born Chinese. I've been referred to as a banana by Overseas Born Chinese (the "real" Chinese)—meaning I was yellow on the outside but white on the inside. The fruit analogy didn't bother me when people called me that in America. But as I sat in the office of the ministry director, meeting Joe for the first time, having just arrived fresh off the plane the day before, I wasn't prepared for what happened next.

"So, I just want to start right off by saying I don't agree with the organization hiring you to work here," Joe said. This was literally the first thing he said to me after the pleasantries of asking how my flight was and the requisite, "How are you?"

I was dumbfounded. I had been recruited by the founder of The Youth Ministry, who spoke at the Christian conference. I had been placed there to develop innovative curriculum for at-risk youth. The founder was especially excited to have me because of my passion and unique ministry skills, training, and the background I brought from the States. But, apparently, Joe did not share the founder's enthusiasm.

I retold this same story to Joe, in hopes of clearing the air. *Perhaps he didn't know my qualifications?*

"I don't care what training you have from the U.S. You are ABC. You are an American. You are not Chinese. You didn't grow up here. Your philosophy and perspectives are Western. What would you know about the struggles of people here?" Joe looked totally peeved, like he had swallowed a fly.

I told him of my summer missions trip in Hong Kong and how I did urban ministry work in the poor working class, inner-city neighborhoods of Sham Shui Po, working with boys from gangs. I spent time traveling from Kowloon to those same neighborhoods in between running camps to tutor English and do Bible studies. But Joe was not persuaded.

"You're not gonna last here. You don't belong here. You should have stayed in the U.S. Why come all the way here?" Joe shrugged his shoulders and shuffled papers at his desk. "Well, if you don't have any questions, I'm going to get back to work."

"So what do you want me to start work on?" I asked.

"Well, the founder stuck you here with me. So I can't do anything about it. But I won't have you working with kids or the curriculum. You can help sweep and clean. Maintenance. That's the best I can give you." Joe turned back to his paperwork.

Now, I am not a quitter, so I figured I'd win Joe over in time. I'd show him I belonged because I was sent. But my determination didn't mean my heart wasn't crushed.

But something was crystal clear to me that moment as I walked out of Joe's office. Being called an American wasn't an insult to me. I felt fiercely protective of the values, dreams, and character that God had formed in me as an American. Being called an American fired me up instead.

When I returned to seeing the kids I had kept in touch with from Sham Shui Po, whom I had served during my summer missions trip, I realized the reason they were drawn so much to the gospel was that it was so unimaginable that an ABC like me would give up my high-tech job and life in the U.S. to come love them. I drew a lot of curiosity from the teens in the neighborhoods because I was the only American they had ever met. They were eager to get together with me, but not to speak Chinese with me. They wanted to learn English and practice speaking English with me! To them, I was 100 percent American, Chinese only by skin color. As far as they were concerned, they were talking to Annie Oakley.

One day, a group of five boys, three of whom were in gangs, suddenly tapped me on the shoulder and said they wanted to take me on a tour of Hong Kong. They were so thankful that I had returned to live in Hong Kong and teach them English and do Bible studies with them, they were all pitching in to treat me to a special meal.

I was filled with anticipation, thrilled with imagining what authentic, hole-in-the wall Hong Kong café or street vendor *dai-pai dong* they were going to take me to! I followed them through streets I would never dare to walk through alone (a murder was committed earlier in the morning in the housing where I had met them that afternoon). After taking multiple bus transfers and subways, we finally ended up in one of the most upscale parts of Hong Kong. They all yelled, "Bonnie-Jeh (Big Sis Bonnie)! Surprise! We're here!" and they opened the door to a McDonald's.

"We thought you miss your food in America! We're treating you to hamburgers and french fries!" They insisted I sit down while they all lined up to order hamburgers and large fries with cups of water.

They sat me down in the middle of the group, squeezing packets of ketchup in the center of the tray. They poured all the fries in one big pile and started digging in.

"Wait!" one of the boys exclaimed, spreading out his arms, keeping eager hands away, protecting our fried potato stash. "Bonnie-Jeh needs to pray, right?"

There, in that McDonald's, squeezed in by my five protectors, I felt like royalty, saying grace for the best-tasting hamburgers and french fries in the whole wide world!

Shortly after the Hong Kong changeover of 1997, The Youth Ministry disbanded all the gospel camps and went from being a nonprofit entity to a for-profit business. Joe finally took me off garbage duty. Why? Because he wanted me to lead leadership training camps for corporations like Chase Manhattan Bank. Finally, the ABC from Silicon Valley with an engineering degree could be of some use to Joe.

Needless to say, I did not go to Hong Kong to lead corporate leadership training camps. The night I finished leading my first leadership training course, I suddenly got a call from the States.

It was Bruce from Silicon Valley.

"Bonnie, I just wanted to check in to see how you're doing. I've been tagged to lead the desktop computing division to support online banking at Wells Fargo Bank. I know it's unlikely, but in case things have changed, I would love to get your help to run that program. You're still in the system on leave of absence."

And that's how I returned back to the States. Because the missionary work I had been called to—the gospel work for which I had been sent by my supporters—had not materialized and The Youth Ministry program was eliminated in exchange for corporate leadership training, I knew it was time to return.

You'd think that after being mistreated and misjudged by someone in authority and shouted down, I might have doubted my worth. It had the opposite effect. Joe's bullying only made me more resolute.

I know who I am. I know my worth. Just because he didn't know my worth didn't change the truth of my value.

I returned more self-assured than I left, a mixture of cultural heritages—a quality of my American identity of which I was now fiercely protective. America is a rich tradition of many races.

I wasn't ashamed of returning to America. The apostle Paul himself had to be lowered in a basket to escape the people who were so angry at him for preaching the gospel that they wanted to stone him. They wanted to silence him.

I had fulfilled my mission. Though Joe had tried to stop the gospel work God had sent me to do by having me pick up trash, God is too powerful to have anyone stop His love. By the time I had left Hong Kong, young people in Sham Shui Po had been baptized, and my sweet kids had memories of Bonnie-Jeh. I left Hong Kong with both happy memories and sad ones.

I no longer wondered if I was Chinese or American. Having lived in Hong Kong, I had no doubt I was American. But I am Chinese American—born embracing both cultures.

I returned to work in Silicon Valley, putting on my heels and suit again. But now what?

> No longer will they call you Deserted,
>   or name your land Desolate.
> But you will be called Hephzibah [My delight is in her]…
>   for the Lord will take delight in you (Isaiah 62:4).

LETTER TO MY YOUNGER SELF
You Are Worth Delighting In

Beloved,

When something doesn't turn out like you planned, know that you'll look back one day and see God at work in a different way. Just not in the way you expected.

And when you face rejection, remember that you still have worth even if someone did not recognize your value.

God honors your faithfulness—not any results, appearance, or numbers. God treasures who you are today. Not who you will become tomorrow.

Plans might seem to fail, but God is accomplishing something deeper. He is delighting in you.

HONG KONG BUBBLE WAFFLE

Having grown up Chinatown, I enjoyed a lot of the authentic Chinese foods in America. But one dessert I had for the first time as a missionary was a Hong Kong Bubble Waffle. Given that waffles are my favorite breakfast anyhow, when I saw a street vendor making what looked like a cross between a crepe and a waffle, and out popped an egg-shaped waffle, I was mesmerized!

The honey golden cakes have a crispy shell, but one bite delivers you instant softness. The aromatic batter is cooked into an egg shape over a metal plate. How can something so simple give so much delight? This delicious dessert was invented in 1950, when a grocery shop owner made use of some cracked eggs and mixed in sugar, flour, and evaporated milk. God's stamp of creativity and the love of food is seen in every culture. I believe God delights in waffles, don't you?

————————— **Reflect and Share** —————————

- *What would you tell your younger self about her self-worth in the face of rejection?*

- *What is something new you're learning about yourself, as you find yourself in hard circumstances you didn't anticipate? How has rejection left its mark on you and on how you feel about yourself?*

- *When is a time in your life that things didn't work out the way you planned? How did God still work in your life through it— just not in the way you expected?*

Chapter 15

Limbo

I returned to the States from my stint as a missionary more quietly than I had left. Instead of a large crowd of people waving me off at the departure gate, a faithful handful of friends picked me up at the San Francisco International Terminal.

That night, eating together, spinning dishes of Chinese entrees around a turntable, my heart felt disconnected. My body was there in California, but Silicon Valley felt foreign to me. Just 24 hours earlier, I was living a totally different life in Hong Kong.

I was serving and moving among the young people I had met in the inner-city conclaves of Sham Shui Po, where predominantly low-income families, the elderly, drug addicts, and unskilled laborers comprised a dense and vibrant neighborhood. It was a diverse mix of migrants from rural China, working-class families, and seniors living in cage homes (a type of residence large enough to fit only one bunk bed surrounded by a metal cage), subdivided flats, and public housing projects.

Although my most beloved and treasured gift from serving on the mission field was these beautiful and life-changing friendships forged among the young boys and girls I met there, I was also emotionally drained, carrying the heartbreaking stories of domestic abuse and poverty. After serving on the front lines in Hong Kong, I was undergoing a second culture shock coming back.

I had trouble explaining to my supporters why I left Hong Kong without airing the dirty laundry of The Youth Ministry—how I was emotionally abused and ill-treated, and how the organization betrayed its gospel values and mission after the 1997 China changeover. It was bait and switch, from my point of view. But it was taboo to bad-mouth the ministry where I had served. Plus, I felt a sense of shame. I was still pretty confused about how I could have been 100 percent sure about my calling to serve five years in Hong Kong, only to return in less than a year. My confidence was shaken. How could I have been so wrong about God's calling in my life?

Without having made any personal, peer-to-peer friends in Hong Kong, I had lived a very solitary life. I didn't mind it really because I was always an introvert at home growing up. My prayer life, journaling, and time spent going deep in the Word grew exponentially, as did my joy. In many ways, I was living my dream of serving as a full-time minister, and I relished my monk-like rhythms of service, work, and prayer. I was thrilled to see the gospel flourish in the soil of relationships. But I was very lonely. I didn't fully realize its effect until I returned to the States.

I entered a wilderness of my soul. Even though I was doing everything I was supposed to do—I was successful in my career, working in Silicon Valley leading product teams, delivering first-to-market technology that later evolved to become cloud computing—I felt invisible to myself and others.

I did not know the way ahead. I was barren of certainty, plans, or direction. I didn't know how I ended up there, and I certainly didn't know how to find my way out of this wilderness of loneliness.

• • •

If you stand at the historic San Francisco Ferry Building—which in the 1930s was the second busiest transit terminal in the world—you would see across the water, past Alcatraz, another island that was just as much of a prison to Chinese Americans who were waiting to be released for entry to San Francisco.

Angel Island.

The purpose of this immigration station was to investigate Chinese who had been denied entry due to the Chinese Exclusion Act of 1882. These immigrants weren't treated as Europeans were at Ellis Island. To gain passage and prevent deportation, immigrants had to prove they had husbands or fathers who were American citizens.

Chinese immigrants could be detained for interrogation for weeks or months—sometimes as long as two years. A person's racial identity and social class determined the intensity of the examination. Although many wanted to return home to China instead of waiting while imprisoned, they had no money to return. If you take an Angel Island tour today, you'll see poetry etched into the walls of detention centers by Chinese Americans stuck there.

These early Chinese American immigrants were stuck in limbo. And so was I.

I felt parked, standing still while all my friends were living life and passing me by. Everyone was getting married, having babies, traveling all over the world, while I was stuck at home, needing to financially provide for Ah-Ma and my younger sister, who were both living with me. My younger sister, whom I had hoped would be free to pursue a college degree, returned home without graduating to live with me and Ah-Ma.

Here I was, now taking care of two people, covering expenses for housing, food, clothing, and discretionary spending. Ah-Ma decided to stop working at the hair salon, saying, "You make more money in less than an hour than I make in a week."

I had no idea what to do. This was not the life I had imagined as a twentysomething professional. When I objected to my younger sister moving back in with me without a plan to be self-sustaining, Ah-Ma said, "What? Just because you think you're smarter doesn't mean you're better than your sister!"

I was promoted to working as chief of staff for the VP of network computing, overseeing a portfolio of 50 different product roadmaps at Sun Microsystems. Yet, the minute I stepped back home, it was like stepping into a time machine. Although I was turning 30, my life did not look very different from when I was 17. I was living in my private Sham Shui Po in California. From where I stood, nothing about my life was ever going to change. I was still stuck in the cycle of dysfunctional poverty. This wasn't poverty of finances; it was poverty in spirit. I did not see any hope of changing my family's dysfunctional and toxic codependency.

I was stuck, unable to move forward. In limbo.

• • •

The apostle Paul became a source of inspiration for me again. He was a tentmaker, serving Christ, working an everyday job, yet serving God's people by faith. Since I could not serve God in Hong Kong, then I figured I would serve Him in Silicon Valley.

I left my Chinese church and went to Peninsula Bible Church in Palo Alto, taking Bible study training classes in the evenings there. After all I had lost, one thing did not change: my love for God's Word and His people. I was still drawn to my loving Savior Jesus, and His voice was my North Star.

I knew I had found my new church family the first night I attended a Bible study class there. After class, I went up to the teacher, Rich Carlson, to introduce myself. Rich looked like a young Frank Sinatra who aged better than Old Blue Eyes, because Rich was a retired military veteran who still got up before six in the morning to do his morning run. Rich had soft brown eyes, tip-top hair parted to the side, and a smile that lit up rosy cheeks. You felt like summer came early whenever he said, "Hello!" to you. Rich reminded me of Mr. Rogers, with the grit of a postwar Jimmy Stewart thrown in.

Rich had retired after a life of service as an officer in the Army, having put in years in Europe. Now, he was one of the pastors at the church. It turned out that he had also served as a missionary for many years before returning back to the States.

My eyes welled up with tears and my body started shaking with sobs, like my feet suddenly had touched home soil. I said, "Can I hug you? I'm an ex-missionary too!"

"Well, sure you can! What do you mean *ex*-missionary? Welcome back, soldier!" And he gave me a big bear hug that truly brought me back home to America.

Rich pulled a handkerchief out of nowhere and offered it to me. "So, where did you serve, and how long where you there? What happened?" Rich asked in rapid-fire succession, as stories suddenly tumbled out of me, like water breaking out of a dam. Even though I'm sure Rich probably preferred to pack his stuff and call it a night, he listened to my stories with focused intensity.

I cried and cried some more, my fragmented stories given in the wrong order, doubtful I made any sense. But because he wasn't from my Chinese church community, I felt safe telling him all the sordid details of the organization and the people who had hurt me so deeply. I finally felt free to confide in someone.

"But what eats me up the most is that I feel I've lost my confidence. I've always felt I trusted how I could hear God. But I was so wrong about Hong Kong. Why would He send me there, knowing I would fail?"

Instead of a theological response, Rich asked me, "Tell me more."

He gave me permission to share my deepest fear: "I don't know what my calling is anymore. I was so sure, but now I feel lost. I don't know God's plan for me. I don't know where I belong."

"What do you mean you don't know God's plan?" Rich looked incredulous. He delivered his next words with punctuation and specificity. "You *are already in* God's plan, Bonnie. God's plan is for you to be right here. *You are right where you belong.* Right here is where God is with you, walking with you."

Right then and there, my heart came home. I had found my church family.

I put my Chinese-English Bible away and began closing the chapter of my life lived as Chinese Bonnie. I became American Bonnie in my new church community.

...

I was invited to join Peninsula Bible Church's pastoral ministry intern program, whose alumni include the renowned author and Bible teacher Chuck Swindoll. I thrived in my new church family, creating and leading a flourishing thirties singles ministry called PrimeTime. My life was filled with lots of friends, a rich community life, and service. But I found myself turning 30, and I was still single.

I had not fallen in love. Because that was okay with me, I believed I had the gift of singleness. I was storing up treasures in heaven by loving and serving people. After all, the apostle Paul did say that it would be better to stay single if you could choose it. So I said, "I do. I will serve You single. I prefer it this way anyway." I was comfortable living a life of purpose, serving and loving others until I saw Jesus in heaven. I had gotten used to living lonely, so nothing seemed out of place. I didn't mind it anymore. You can't make someone fall in love with you. And I can't make myself fall in love with anyone, right?

So, what I couldn't control, I didn't worry about. I simply chose to take myself out of the running. I chose to be single.

I didn't know I was really just used to hiding my heart. But God would soon change the identity of loneliness that I wore as my name. God makes a way through the wilderness, and He would make a stream right in the middle of the desert of my loneliness.

He gives us more grace (James 4:6).

LETTER TO MY YOUNGER SELF
You Are Worthy of Grace

Beloved,

Don't be hard on yourself. Be gentle with yourself. Give yourself grace.

You somehow believe you're only valuable to others if you can do something for them. You work really hard to do things right so you don't have to need other people so much.

You're unsure of your calling. But I'm here to tell you that your calling isn't something that you do for others or even do for God.

Your calling is to live by grace.

You don't have to earn God's care and attention. Jesus is the friend who always smiles, just being near you. Your true calling is simply to let God love you more every day.

That's it.

THE CHURCH IN CHINESE HISTORY

The earliest mention of Christianity in Chinese documents dates back to the seventh century, taking root later in the sixteenth century when Jesuit missionaries arrived. In 1807, Protestant missionary work began with Robert Morrison, who later produced a Chinese translation of the Bible that took 12 years to complete. The most famous missionary to China was Hudson Taylor, sent by China Inland Mission in 1866, whose vision was to help nurture a Chinese church led by native Chinese believers instead of nonnative missionaries. Over 8,500 Protestant missionaries served in China during that period.[1]

Hudson Taylor has been described as soft-spoken and shy, with a gentle spirit. God used Hudson's gracious way to touch the hearts of people who longed to know God in a personal way. As evidenced through centuries of missionaries putting love into action by serving the poor and overlooked in society, grace is what changes hearts, sparking faith to believe God's love is real. But how can you continuously give what you don't first receive yourself? So, when you're feeling stressed or self-doubt troubles you, it's okay. Give yourself the grace Jesus offers for you to freely receive.

Reflect and Share

- *What would you tell your younger self about her desire for attention and care?*

- *Are you in a season of limbo? How is God reassuring you that His presence is still with you, even in the confusion?*

- *When in your life did you feel in limbo? Who helped you see God's presence in your life? Looking back, what was the purpose of that season, and what did you gain?*

Chapter 16

Red Bean Dessert

E ric didn't understand how beans could end up being a dessert.
Even though it wasn't quite time for a midafternoon snack, we walked past a Hong Kong style café, and I couldn't resist. I grabbed him by the hand to pull him through the doorway. "C'mon! They have my favorite thing ever—*hong dou bing* (紅豆冰)—Red Bean Ice!" This was one of my favorite desserts growing up in Chinatown. My first memory of a summer dessert isn't a melting popsicle, but a trip to the local *Cha Chaan Teng*—a Hong Kong style café.

"What is this now?" Eric asked, which is a common phrase I heard as his cultural attaché on our Asian culinary adventures. I hurried to get in a long line. This was the first rule of queueing I had learned as a Chinese girl: *If you see a line, get in it first, ask questions later.*

Even though Chinese people name their dishes by describing the ingredients rather than by knighting them with a name, Eric needed more info.

"Think of it as a red bean slushie," I replied, which solicited a quizzical expression from him. "It's like a red bean frappuccino or a root beer float, except there are real pieces of red beans mushed in!" I explained.

"In other words, it's totally not like any of those things," Eric replied dryly, chuckling.

Fifteen minutes later, we were sitting at the table with this classic Cantonese red bean ice drink, which came into popularity during my childhood in the '70s and originated from the Cha Chaan Tengs that immigrants like my parents frequented when back home.

"I mean, I like beans as much as anybody else," Eric offered. "I do like chili." He flashed his boyish grin, looking hesitantly at the tall fountain drink filled with red bean mash and topped with three inches of shaved ice and a swirl of condensed milk.

"Just think of it as a red bean malt shake," I laughed.

Eric gave me a thumbs-up. "Sounds delicious!"

Part of the fun of enjoying this treat is that it's a two-hand operation. You take a long spoon in one hand to scoop out the beans and crushed ice, and with the other, you sip sweetness through a straw. This dessert is something you drink and eat at the same time. How fun is that, right?

After a few courtesy bites, Eric slid the dessert back to me. "You enjoy, honey. I'm good." I was undeterred. We'll just have to come back again. Over time, he'll learn to like it.

* * *

Food has been the one thing I fully embrace about my Chinese heritage. Enjoying food has always meant sharing love and connection.

Growing up in my Chinese culture, when friends greeted each other, we didn't say, "How are you?" We said, "Have you eaten yet?" Friends, classmates, neighbors, and even new acquaintances—we greet one another by making sure everyone has eaten. If they haven't, you immediately open your cupboards or fridge. You find something to eat because it's a joy and honor for someone to enjoy a meal in your home, not an inconvenience.

Now, if you happen to be visiting with friends at your home in the afternoon, it's perfectly normal to spontaneously invite them to stay for dinner. If you've already taken meat out to thaw for a meal, you adjust your plans. You have your friends stay, and you set the table with extra rice bowls and sets of chopsticks.

Food is wellness, life, and care.

I wasn't the only one serving as a cultural attaché to Eric. It went both ways. When we dated, Eric made all the American foods like pancakes, baked chicken, and chili. The only American dish I knew how to cook was spaghetti. So, when we got married, I thought I'd impress him with my culinary spaghetti skills. As the pasta was boiling, I set a second pot on a burner and poured in a jar of Ragu spaghetti sauce. I chopped onions and mixed in ground beef. But to Eric's horror, he saw me dump the raw ground beef directly into the bubbling red sauce.

"Um… honey," Eric began cautiously. "Don't you brown the beef first?"

"Why would I do that?" I said as I stirred. "This is much faster."

"How are you going to know if the beef is cooked through in the sauce?" Eric was worried we'd get salmonella poisoning.

"Eric. I've been cooking spaghetti this way for years! You'll be fine," I laughed because I'd never seen him look so disturbed.

We were newlyweds, so he said, "Okay, honey. Just think about it."

• • •

We came from two different worlds. His culture and upbringing did not fit into mine. I was waiting for someone to fit into my Chinese cultural heritage and embrace the idea that family came in a three-for-one instant family package, with mom and sister in tow.

The thing I didn't count on was meeting Eric. He was not a potential match for the dutiful Chinese daughter.

So, you can imagine how peculiar it was dating Eric. He was a blond-haired, blue-eyed boy, who grew up in a small town where he biked to school with the smell of the pulp mill filling the air. Then he found his way to working in high tech in Silicon Valley after serving in the U.S. Army. He wasn't familiar with my family's Chinese customs or traditions. He didn't speak the language. He was the furthest thing from what I considered as a candidate for marriage.

So, when Eric walked in one night as I was emceeing the weekly gathering for thirtysomethings at our church, I didn't even consider him a possibility. He attended another church in the area, but a friend invited him to check out our group. Afterward, some of us decided to go grab some late-night food at a Chinese restaurant. Eric came along as a newcomer.

We were seated around a big round table, and since we were eating family style, we were calling out names of our entrée picks like placing bets at a poker table. I opened by declaring my dish, which prompted Eric—who sat clear across the table from me—to look up from his menu. The first question Eric asked me was, "What is beef chow fun?" This was my favorite dish as a child, and anyone who is familiar with Chinese cuisine knows that beef chow fun is a standard dish.

The fact that he didn't even know what this was—and I later found out he'd never even had dim sum—made me highly doubtful he could be The One. The odds of this ever working out were nil.

● ● ●

When I logged onto my email the next day, I found something unexpected in my inbox. It was a short email from Eric, thanking me for welcoming him to the group and saying how much he'd enjoyed visiting. I responded with a standard reply a group leader gives to a newcomer. What was even more peculiar was that after this first email, I found a new note in my inbox from Eric every day—for a month.

That very short first email grew into a series of daily digital letters we wrote each other, growing longer with each exchange. With each subsequent message, a most unusual feeling sparked in me. I was intrigued.

I had never felt so captivated as we wrote each other in the quietness of our shared solitude. Opening each letter started an overwhelming peace washing over me, like stumbling upon something beautifully wild in natural form. To be let into someone's soul is discovering a serenity that makes you wonder how you could be so lucky.

Though we came from two very different worlds, writing letters to each other unlocked an intimacy I had never experienced before. The astonishing wonder of it all was finding I could enter into his inner world too.

Like moonlight calling to the ocean's tides, as gravity tugs on the earth and its waters move in response, our two souls in solitude were being drawn to each other.

• • •

Was I falling in love with Eric? I couldn't be sure. I finally had found someone who spoke the soul language of words. But choosing to write a new story with Eric would mean I needed to choose my own path that was separate from my mother's Chinese world.

Should I choose to write a new story with Eric, or stay in the script I was born into with Ah-Ma?

It would mean my story would involve some leaving to make room for some coming home. To start a new chapter in my life, I would need to say goodbye. But it began in the most unexpected way. With an earthquake that destroyed and crumbled life as I've always known it.

> Now thanks be to God who always leads us in triumph in Christ, and through us diffuses the fragrance of His knowledge in every place. For we are to God the fragrance of Christ among those who are being saved and among those who are perishing (2 Corinthians 2:14-15 NKJV).

LETTER TO MY YOUNGER SELF
You Are Worthy to Choose Your Own Path

Beloved,

You can't embrace how you are beloved when you follow some-one else's path. You are worthy to live your own version of a beautiful life.

Do not give up on yourself. God's not giving up on you. You only see walls of impossibility, but God plan is something you will see later by putting your trust in Him and taking action to change today.

You are waiting for things to fit into your plans. But God will change your life so that His plan unfolds in ways you can't see.

God completes you not by the sameness of cultures, but as the Holy Spirit connects you to others through shared human experiences. Diversity brings richness.

THE ART OF CANTONESE CUISINE

Cantonese cuisine is from the Guangdong province, along the southern coastal region of China, which includes Hong Kong, where my parents are from. Because it was the first region opened for trade by the Qing Dynasty Imperial Court in the eighteenth century, Cantonese cooking became the first cosmopolitan cuisine that travelers enjoyed in China. Because early immigrants came from Guangdong, American's first taste of Chinese food became Cantonese cuisine.[1]

One important secret to cooking my childhood Cantonese dish called beef chow fun is to obtain a smoky flavor from stir-frying the noodles *in a seasoned wok.* The seasoning is *wok hei,* literally, "breath of the wok." This wok hei is the patina created from the caramelization of sugars, foods, and oils absorbed into the wok over time, based on the foods that have been cooked in it. The wok hei is unique—a reflection of the wok's history. Wok hei gives food an indelible aroma that is unique to each wok's culinary experiences.

In the same way, each of us carries the breath of God, the Holy Spirit, adding flavor into the world through our unique history and experiences that are unmistakably ours. The diversity of family traditions and cultural experiences is what gives each of us the fragrance of Christ.

As Jesus said, "You are the salt of the earth." Your seasoned life is what creates your future, as you make sense of your past so you can live fully in the present. Free to choose your own path.

------------------------------ **Reflect and Share** ------------------------------

- *What would you say to your younger self about choosing her own path?*

- *How is God inviting you to connect with someone who might seem different from you? How might your differences enrich your life?*

- *How is God inviting you to change your plans by challenging your ideas of what is possible or impossible?*

Chapter 17

Earthquake

In 1906, a devastating earthquake destroyed over 80 percent of the city of San Francisco. Chinatown was leveled. The city made plans to upend and move all Chinese residents to the outskirts of the city, relegating them to the most undesirable part of town. But quick-thinking leaders of Chinatown approached the government, suggesting that Chinatown be rebuilt as a tourist-friendly neighborhood. They brought business to the city, and the community flourished. Life was rebuilt and remade.[1]

In the same way, an earthquake that would level life as I knew it would also enter my story. But, unlike the leaders of Chinatown, I had no idea how I could ever recover from the devastation of losing everything I had worked so hard to build. There were no tremors that warned me of impending ruin one warm evening in spring.

He was holding me close to him to say goodnight. The night sky hung above us, the air was crisp, and the nearby blossoming trees gave the breeze a sweetness as I laid my head on his shoulder.

The moment was ripe for drawing near to each other in tenderness and affection.

We were inseparable. Maybe because we had already been writing to each other for a month, it seemed we just couldn't talk fast enough, making up for lost time—for all the years that we'd been separated in our whole lives.

Tonight was special because Eric had invited me over to his apartment and made dinner. I was impressed. Not only because he prepared *adename* for appetizers—baked chicken with a teriyaki glaze—and actually served decent steamed rice, but he even lit a candle at our table.

This guy seemed too good to be true. I was waiting for the other shoe to drop. But I hoped it wouldn't be that night.

Please just let me enjoy this daydream for a little longer, I whispered to myself. *Let me just enjoy this spell of a romance, before my carriage turns into a pumpkin, my dress back to rags, and the footman turns into a mouse.*

Honestly, it seemed like we were as different as night and day. Eric was as American as apple pie. Born and raised in a small town in Washington State, Eric worked as a Russian linguist in the Army before he came out to California to work in high tech, following a family tradition of military service. His father, Butch, is a Purple Heart veteran who fought in the Vietnam War, having survived behind enemy lines for two weeks until a chopper came to get him and his squad out. His grandfather, who hailed from Arkansas, served in the Navy during the Korean War.

Me? Anything I knew about the military I got from watching *A Few Good Men*. And just once, and only once, I watched *Full Metal Jacket*—mostly through the gaps between the fingers of my hands covering my eyes when it aired on cable TV.

But all these thoughts fell to the wayside when we snuggled on the couch after dinner, looking through photo albums, swapping notes on Eric's travels in the Army and my adventures as a California girl, and how we'd missed each other like ships passing in the night. Just a few months after Eric drove to California for the first time with his belongings in a U-Haul, I boarded a plane and left for Hong Kong. I felt close to him, listening to his sandy-soft voice, reliving memories together—when he reached over to the coffee table to retrieve a gift for me.

He had burned a CD of songs dedicated to me.

It was a mix tape! I felt like we traveled back in a time machine and were teenagers back in the '80s. I felt something I had never felt before: I was happy.

He got up and popped the CD into the player. He pulled me up off the sofa with one hand and said, "Would you like to dance?" There, in his little apartment, we danced to "Amen Kind of Love," by Daryle Singletary, which I had never heard before. I couldn't stop laughing.

"What's so funny?" Eric asked, laughing along as he tried to teach me the two-step, which is apparently the most basic, bread-and-butter country dance move. I still somehow managed to botch it. I was out of my element, transported into some imaginary country-western dance floor, and I loved feeling quite literally swept off my feet.

It could have been a perfect ending to a magical night as we held each other in the parking lot to say goodnight. I could sense what was about to happen next, as Eric drew me close to him. Slowly, gently, he nestled me in even closer. To kiss me.

But I was afraid. How would I know if I could really trust him? I couldn't tell him that *an unspeakable trauma* once happened to me. I was wrong once. What if I was wrong again? How serious was this really going to be? Nothing good ever lasted for me. Why would this be different? I didn't want him to think I didn't want to kiss him. But I also didn't want any more memories of kisses that never stayed.

"I'm sorry." I turned away, awkwardly fumbling for what to say next.

"What is it?" Eric asked.

"No, I want to, but…" I didn't want to say too much, but was fearful I wasn't saying enough. "It's complicated." As soon as those words left my lips, I felt my chances for love slip away. I was ruining the moment.

"Shh…" Eric whispered, gathering me closer. "You don't have to worry about a thing. Just let me love you." Then he simply held me.

We stood there, entwined in the quietness, before he tucked me in my car, and I drove into the night.

That was the very moment when I knew that life was going to be different. When I knew that he was the one. I felt safe in his arms.

Everything I thought I knew about my heart shifted. Walls crumbled down, decimated in a matter of seconds, and the fortress I had constructed where I hid in safety all my life was breached. The moment felt like an earthquake, shaking me to the core, with seismic waves of excitement mixed with dread leveling the landscape of my life to the ground.

Like the 1906 earthquake that destroyed Chinatown, my life would soon be turned upside down in order for God to remake and rebuild a new life for me where love would stay.

I could hold on to who I was and not let this moment change me. I could just sit and wait for what I felt was safe, familiar, and not messy. I could stay where I was and hope to feel something again one day when I was more sure of myself and what it would mean to fall in love.

I had always assumed I would date and marry someone who could live with me in Ah-Ma's world. But how could Eric fit into my life with Ah-Ma?

The journey ahead would not be easy.

Life is not a fairy tale.

Did you know that after the earthquake of 1906 leveled the city, the resulting fires that burned out of control were even more destructive, engulfing whatever was left standing? The city lay barren, laden with debris. The city was covered in ash.

But this is what God does best. He makes beauty out of ashes.

> For those who grieve in Zion—to bestow on them a crown of beauty instead of ashes, the oil of joy instead of mourning, and a garment of praise instead of a spirit of despair (Isaiah 61:3).

 ## LETTER TO MY YOUNGER SELF
Beauty for Ashes Will Be Your Crown

Beloved,

Love isn't going to come the way you expect it.

Beauty for ashes will be your crown displaying God's splendor.

Keep holding on to the things you value in a relationship. Be more honest than you might feel comfortable with because then your whole heart can truly be present. Take the risk to believe the love you desire is something someone else wants to experience with you.

Never give up on finding love because it will keep you tender, vulnerable, and open. Ask Him to bring someone into your life who can be His heart and hands to express that love to you.

The dreams you dare to whisper in private, God hears. You are not forgotten. With God, all things are possible.

CHINESE BRUSH PAINTING

Chinese brush painting is one of the oldest continuous artistic traditions in the world. It uses calligraphy techniques of brush and ink instead of oil paints. In Chinese classical paintings, artwork from the Tang Dynasty (AD 618–907) depicting landscapes called *shanshui* (山水—"mountain water") weren't created for visual representation. Instead, the goal was to express symbols to reflect the artist's heart and mind.[2]

For example, Emperor Huizong created a painting called *Birds in a Blossom Plum Tree* with two birds resting on a tree branch together, symbolizing faithful love and marriage. A Chinese poem notes: "I wish for a lover in whose heart I alone exist," with an allusion to two birds. Across every culture, we see that the universal language of the soul is love. For we are made in God's image, and God is love.

--------- **Reflect and Share** ---------

- *What would you tell your younger self about finding love?*

- *How is God guiding you to deeper vulnerability in your relationships and being more honest about your emotional desire or needs? How is God inviting you to let others love you?*

- *If you are single, what experiences in dating helped shape the things you desire in a relationship? What are those? If you are married, what experiences helped you know your spouse was the one?*

Chapter 18

Cut Up

It was supposed to be a simple road trip. To go down south to Los Angeles and ride roller coasters at Six Flags Magic Mountain with Eric and some friends from church. A long weekend was coming up, the Fourth of July, and everyone thought it would be a great way to spend the three-day vacation together.

"Yeah! Let's go!" Eric thought it was a fun idea. Wasn't it?

For everyone else in the group, it was no big deal. Except for me.

The embarrassing private truth I had never told anyone was this: I was 31 years old, and I had never spent a July Fourth weekend or any holiday away from Ah-Ma. I never went anywhere if it wasn't traveling for work or a ministry event. That's because I always needed to stay home with Ah-Ma.

Here I was in my thirties, shepherding our church's singles ministry, a Silicon Valley high-tech professional leading teams and flying across the country for business one week in Boston, the next week meeting up with engineers in Fort Lauderdale, then stopping by our data center in Broomfield, Colorado, before swinging back home. So, how could I tell Eric or anyone else in my life that every weekend and on every holiday I never stepped more than a few feet away from Ah-Ma? How could I tell them I was deathly afraid of my mother, and I had to ask for my mother's permission to go out? How could I explain that a grown-up, educated, career woman like me was required to spend my weekends taking Ah-Ma grocery shopping, clothes shopping, eating out, or accompanying her on day trips to the beach? If I didn't, I'd be branded selfish and get yelled at for hours or have dinner thrown into the sink because I had done something to upset her.

Holidays were especially important to Ah-Ma. "I'm not a dog you leave alone at home while you go out and have fun with your friends," Ah-Ma said. "When you were little, I could have left you and your sister and lived my own life. I could have had a lot more money, free to do whatever I please. I could've given you up at an orphanage. Remember, Bonnie. I'm your mother."

I always begged her, "Ah-Ma. Please stop. Don't be like this. I can't be happy knowing you're unhappy and alone." Our conversations always ended the same way: "I won't go. I'll stay here with you."

So when I told Eric, "I'm not sure if I can go," he grew concerned and asked me, "Why?" Usually people respected the vague answers I gave. I'd just end up not joining.

Do I lie to Eric? Will I take this moment of potential happiness and step toward it? Or do I turn back, like I always have?

I hadn't a single clue how I would get Ah-Ma to let me go, but I found myself answering, "Never mind. Let's go. We'll have fun."

Eric broke into a smile. But a feeling of panic dropped into my gut and did not go away. It settled there like a tremor—a telltale sign that something bad was about to happen.

● ● ●

The truth is, my mother would disappear for hours all the time when I was a little girl, leaving me terrified out of my mind. Ah-Ma would start screaming at me, then slam the door on the way out so hard that the windows would rattle violently, as if the walls would fall down on my head. I'd hear her turn the ignition to start the car engine, followed by the sound of her tires peeling out of the driveway.

Each time when she left in a rage at night, I was all alone, having to calm my little sister and make up a reason why Ah-Ma had left us in an empty house for hours, never knowing when or if she was coming back. I'd walk around like a homeless person from room to room, not knowing what to do or where to go. I could only sit by the window, looking for Ah-Ma to return. Loneliness wrapped around my heart like a cocoon. All alone.

I got used to living in this cocoon. It became my safety, my home. I befriended my solitude, grew familiar with my walls, and learned to fill it with good things like duty, prayer, books, school, ministry, and work. I grew to not mind it so much and survived many winters this way.

But that night, as I considered joining Eric for a road trip south, the cocoon I had created to protect my heart was changing into something different and new. The loneliness became threads of silk God was using to weave something beautiful. God was clothing my heart with a new desire. He was weaving the tapestry of a new story.

The loneliness I had endured was teaching me that it was there for a reason. The ache was telling me I had a need. My heart was coming alive. I whispered for the first time, *I don't want to be alone anymore.* I wanted to be loved more than I wanted to hide.

We weren't created to stay in our cocoons. What once brought us protection and safety was only a temporary sanctuary that God provided by His grace.

Was spring here? I wanted someone to love me the way I longed to be loved. Was it possible? I didn't know. But I wanted to write a new story with what my brokenness had taught me in the winter.

Although caterpillars become butterflies in the spring, they must first survive the cold winter. They must find protection in the safety of a cocoon.

* * *

I was standing in front of my sliding mirror closet door in my bedroom the night before Eric was set to pick me up in the morning for the road trip. My arms worked like a rotating easel, holding up one garment at a time like it was a painting soon to be framed for viewing along a gallery wall. I was trying to decide which summer dresses looked prettier, yet would avoid giving the message that I was trying too hard to impress.

I was counting on my fingers how many days' worth of outfits I needed, being careful to avoid packing like I'd thrown in the kitchen sink, when my quiet reverie suddenly collapsed. The door exploded open, sending a lightning bolt of terror through my pounding heart.

The force of the door being punched open smacked so hard against the wall that the doorknob boomeranged back, ricocheting off the foreboding figure looming in the doorway. I felt I was seven years old, and my breath splintered.

Ah-Ma was livid. Her shoulders heaved, and her breath teetered on the edge between measured and seething as her jaw squared like the head of a sledgehammer. Her arms shot out, flailing like an enraged conductor orchestrating a perfect storm of outrage. The ocean of anger fuming inside her boiled with the volcanic lash of her words.

"So you're *really* going to go? You're going to leave me here for *him*?" she thundered, as her eyes narrowed into me. She wouldn't even say his name.

"Ah-Ma! I'm not just going with Eric. There are friends. From church," I pleaded.

"How convenient," she countered. "How long have you known him? A few sweet-sounding words, and you're all his? So easy. So cheap. Why are you so desperate?" She let out a big sigh, shaking her head like I was a lost cause.

I didn't know what to say. The thought of Eric's intimate words— *Just let me love you*—suddenly made me feel shameful. I began to doubt whether I had only imagined there was something more than superficial attraction between Eric and me. I wondered if my recently growing loneliness was simply making me desperate. And I began to feel cheap.

"Did it occur to you that he's just in it for fun? He doesn't care about you. He doesn't even know you!" Ah-Ma was speaking like she was explaining the ABCs. "Just watch. Once he finds out you have to take care of me, you'll see. He'll leave."

"Ah-Ma, this is just a simple, fun weekend to go ride roller coasters. I haven't dated anyone since college. I'm 31 years old, Ah-Ma. Maybe you're right. It won't last. But I like Eric. I won't know if I don't try. I've taken care of you my whole life. Why can't you be happy for me?"

I started crying because I was more scared than anything. Scared that I'd said it so bluntly. Scared because I had never spoken to my mom like this.

"How stupid can you be? A man comes along and pays you a little attention—and you think that makes you special?" Ah-Ma scoffed. "You've forgotten who you are, Bonnie Lee! You're *my* daughter. You belong to *me*!" Ah-Ma screamed at the top of her lungs, her eyes wild with rage, wailing with all her might, like she was blowing all the air out of her lungs, her face turning purple, her hands balled into fists.

If I thought I was scared before, I was beyond terrified now. I felt as if I had been teleported into another dimension, in a horror movie where the screen goes berserk and the screen goes into a fuzzy filter. I had never seen my mother shake with such rage against me. I stood there defenseless, steeling my heart against the barrage of insults she had rained on me. I thought she would storm out, and I would hear her grab her car keys and slam the front door, as she would often do, leaving me behind.

Instead, Ah-Ma tore out, thundering into the kitchen. I heard drawers opening and slamming shut. The next thing I knew, she flew back into the room with the glint of steel, brandishing a large pair of scissors in her hand.

She shoved my sliding closet doors open, violently yanking my clothes off the hangers. She was shaking as she pulled apart my clothes by the neck openings to tear them up, simultaneously, wildly, haphazardly cutting up my clothes, running the blade of the shears against my clothes with one hand, tugging at them like she was strangling the life out of them.

"Everything you have, EVERYTHING you are is because of me! If it weren't for me, there would be no you!" Ah-Ma screamed each line as she clawed at my desk, clutching whatever she could get her hands on, ejecting my books, notebooks, knickknacks, swiping things off, throwing them all over my room as confetti of fury.

I stood there, choking in my tears, afraid to move or breathe. Frozen and paralyzed.

Confusion engulfed me. I just wanted to ride roller coasters with a boy I liked who liked me too. *How can something so simple become so very wrong?*

A thought hit me like a siren: *Something is really, really wrong.*

I looked at the blade of her shears. Ah-Ma had told me earlier in the week—when I asked her for permission to go on the road trip—that if I dared to leave her that weekend, she would kill herself. "You'll come back and find me dead," she threatened. "You'll never have peace. It's either him or me."

I was afraid she would hurt me. The thought flashed through my mind—*She's going to end things once and for all. Ah-Ma thought I wouldn't go. But I called her bluff, and now, if she can't be happy, she'll take my happiness too.*

She might kill me and take me with her.

That's what fear does to your mind. You don't think rationally. You don't think, "My mother would never do that. People say things in anger. They don't mean it."

So I ran to the bathroom and locked the door.

This only made Ah-Ma bang on the door and yell louder, adding fuel to the fire of her anger. "You good-for-nothing! You're not leaving me!"

I sat on top of the bathroom vanity, looking into the mirror, saying to myself, *This is not normal. I am 31 years old.*

This is the day I choose whom I will serve. This can't be why God created me—to hide in my bathroom, fearful of my mother, fearful to choose my chance of happiness.

I serve a God of peace, who loves me.

Was I my mother's daughter or my Heavenly Father's daughter? Did I really believe I was God's beloved?

This can't be how the daughter of the King should live, in fear.

I have to leave.

I have to change my story.

> Even if my father and mother abandon me, the LORD will take care of me (Psalm 27:10 GOD'S WORD).

 ## LETTER TO MY YOUNGER SELF
You Are Worthy of Peace

Beloved,

You will have to make a very hard decision one day to choose peace over fear. You'll have to keep choosing to believe you are worthy of that peace.

You will have to leave, even though you've given your all to stay.

Peace isn't freedom from conflict. Peace is trusting God enough to make the right choice in the midst of conflict. Choosing peace will mean you need to let go of someone you've held onto in order to take the hand of God, who promises to lead you beside quiet waters.

You will need to count the cost and set your face like flint to leave what isn't healthy. Because to continue staying with someone who is abusing you emotionally, toxic to your well-being, hurting your body, heart, and soul is breaking the heart of God.

To choose peace, you will need to be honest with yourself. There will come a time for this honesty, and that time will be now.

CHINESE POETRY

In Chinese culture, poetry has been a central way to express private and intense emotion, giving insight into the inner life of Chinese writers since the first millennium BC. Chinese poetry is intricately intertwined with the art of calligraphy and painting. Poetry shows up on painted scrolls as a way to express an artist's heart through calligraphy. Even the way a calligrapher writes the characters in a poem conveys tremendous meaning and depth.

Through the safety of metaphor, the expression of emotion brings peace when hearts are torn in anguish. It's fascinating to see poetry reflected as a universal human expression—from King Solomon in Ecclesiastes to a Chinese poet in the Han Dynasty, praying to God to find true love in the poem "By Heaven!"

Reflect and Share

- *What would you tell your younger self about navigating family dysfunction, emotional health, and creating boundaries between adult children and parents?*

- *How is God guiding you to make changes in your family dynamics so that your well-being is preserved?*

- *What was your relationship with your mother like when you were a child? If she is still living, how does it compare with your relationship with her now that you're an adult? How has your mother-daughter relationship influenced the way you make decisions?*

Chapter 19

Family Code

Ah-Ma kept pounding on the door of the bathroom, where I had retreated to hide from her, and she would not stop. Ah-Ma was furious, screaming, "Come out! Come out!" But I would not let her hurt me.

I stared, crying in the mirror, asking God, "What do I do?"

This wasn't the first time I had locked myself in the bathroom to escape from Ah-Ma, waiting until I heard her go back to her bedroom. I'd listen for her pacing up and down the hallway to stop, before knowing it was safe to emerge.

But that night, Ah-Ma was not giving up.

"Well, if I can't sleep tonight, you're not going to sleep either!" She spent the entire night making a racket, talking to herself at times, then spiking into sudden outbursts outside the bathroom door, pounding and screaming again.

She was furious that I wasn't conceding as I usually did.

"If you go, you'll come home to find me in a pool of blood," she promised. "Then you'll be sorry. You'll always have that image burned into your mind. What you did to your own mother!"

She knew the potency of such a threat. She was taking away the one thing I always desperately wanted: home. She knew cutting up my clothes would scare me. She had violated my space, and now, Ah-Ma went for the nuclear option. *She would take away my home.*

Home. Home is the universal need we all long to have met. Home is something everyone understands, dreams of, guards with their life, and is broken over losing.

Unlike all the other times, I decided to wait her out. My strategy was that no matter what, I had to leave on the road trip the next morning with Eric. It wasn't even about Eric anymore. It was a matter of who I belonged to: God or Ah-Ma?

This wasn't a strategy I came up with on my own. This is what two people I had decided to confide in had counseled me to do.

Unbeknownst to Ah-Ma, earlier in the week, when I initially asked her for permission to go on the road trip and she responded by threatening suicide, I did something I had never done before. Ironically, it was Ah-Ma who drove me to break the family code of silence she'd been teaching me to keep my whole life.

I told someone what was happening.

Because this was the first time Ah-Ma had threatened to harm herself, the imminent danger was so alarming, I seriously worried about my mother's mental health. I couldn't bear the responsibility of anything tragic happening on my watch. I didn't want to be on the six o'clock news one day. I needed to get counsel on how to help Ah-Ma.

So I decided to call Carol, my community life pastor, who was overseeing me as I led the singles ministry at church. I trusted her instinctively because of her vulnerability and honesty. About a year ago, during one of our weekly lunches after talking about ministry, I began confiding to Carol about some of the crazy happenings inside my family for the first time in my life.

I was calling more for my mother than for myself. Carol conferenced in our church's senior pastor, Doug Goins, to confer in the matter.

Oh, no! I thought. *Not the lead pastor!* Suddenly, I went from scared sick to panicked. But I'll remember what Doug said to me my whole life, as clearly as the day I accepted Christ as a little girl.

It was the first time I had ever told other human, real persons (other than God) about the codependency, the dysfunction that went on in our house, the rages, how I had been supporting both my mother and sister financially for years, and how I had to get permission to go out with my friends.

I was so nervous pouring out these shameful secrets. My whole body was shaking, and my teeth were chattering. *There goes my leadership position at church,* I thought. *Now, my pastors will think I'm officially messed up.* I figured they would politely refer me to the local counseling offices, give me a list of trained counselors and therapists, and advise me to make an appointment.

Instead, Doug said, "Bonnie, have you ever heard of Narcissistic Personality Disorder?"

"No, I haven't," I answered. "What is it?"

Here we go, I thought. *I'm gonna get labeled.* Talk about an oversharing hangover! I was already beating myself up for thinking anybody was going to understand this mess of my life. I immediately regretted calling Carol. I was preparing to say thank you and I appreciate everything very much and hightail it out of there.

"NPD is a real mental disorder," Doug said slowly. "And I'm saying this as lovingly as I can, but truthfully. I really think *your mom* has NPD."

Seismic waves. Magnitude of 7.1 shook my entire world in that moment. *What? Excuse me?*

"Bonnie, you do not belong to your mother. You belong to God. You are God's daughter," Doug said. "God brought Eric into your life, and if he invited you to go to Magic Mountain, you don't need your mother's permission. I want you to go, no matter what."

I was shocked. Wasn't Doug going to preach to me about honoring my mother? And tell me it would be better if I stayed?

"But she says she'll kill herself if I choose Eric over her," I said. I was thinking, *Doug, you don't know my mom. She'll do it.* "I can't carry the weight of that guilt."

Doug asked some probing questions, based on his decades of experience counseling victims of abuse, and the wisdom gained from walking people through complicated, dysfunctional family dynamics in his years of pastoring. I shared more with Doug about the intricacies of what had happened, leading up to the recent events. Carol also filled in the blanks, adding her insight and assessment of the situation since I'd been confiding in her about my mother for some time.

"Well, tell you what, Bonnie. Your mom is not the one I'm worried about. She is a very powerful woman if she can get a 31-year-old to do what she wants. I'm worried about *you*. Your mother, a narcissist, is not going to kill herself." Doug was adamant.

"But what if she does?" I wasn't convinced.

Then Doug said. "She has always used fear to control you. Your mother does not own you. If your mom decides to kill herself, that's between her and God. If she kills herself, I will officiate the funeral. That's how positive I am she will not end her life." He wasn't kidding.

Carol had also confided her own story. As a little girl, her uncle had played a "game" and cut her wrist. She was so afraid of the blood staining the carpet that she stayed quiet and didn't tell anyone. "If someone asked me, 'Do you have abuse in your family?' I would've said no. If you're raised with this stuff, you don't recognize it." She told me victims will often choose not to testify against their physical, emotional, or sexual abusers because they think, "It was my stupid fault to begin with. It's not their fault. It was me letting it happen."

Carol said this wasn't about the road trip anymore. It was about control. If I didn't take this step to Eric, I would be stuck in Ah-Ma's control. She told me, "God wants you to step into the newness. I'm sorry it's so scary and messy. I wish there were an easier way. But just because something is hard doesn't make it wrong. There is power in stepping over the shame. You are safe, and you can walk out of this," Carol assured me.

I thought so much of the dysfunction in my family was cultural because I was Chinese. But as I held the phone with tears streaming down my face, listening to Carol and Doug—neither of whom was Asian—I realized the prison I had been living in was not about the color of my cultural heritage. The culture of loneliness I felt was universal, resulting from living in a broken world of lonely people. But because of God's love, we are rescued from loneliness the moment we turn to each other and carry one another's burdens.

It is not good for man or woman to be alone. It is not good for any of us to be alone.

I suddenly found myself transported into a brand-new kingdom where people were no longer separated from each other because of shame, secrets, or brokenness. In this new kingdom, there was no need to keep secrets from each other because everyone felt connected to each other by the truth, not by shame. The kingdom had a new family code: It is the very flaws we all carry that bring us together as brothers and sisters, so that we can see God in all the glorious ways He loves, rescues, accepts, and welcomes us, just as we are. Our flaws become beautiful because they draw us to love each other even more deeply.

An overwhelming sense of acceptance washed over me. No more hiding. I was not alone anymore. God's love and grace had a face and a name. Doug and Carol knew my name and understood my pain. They accepted me even as I shared my shame.

God was bringing me into a new kind of family—one that wasn't knit together by a common color, culture, nationality, or economic status, high or low. I could live by a new family code with God as my Heavenly Father. This family code was founded in light, rooted in love, abounding in grace, and nurtured by faith and freedom.

This spiritual family crosses all cultures. This true family was born out of a living faith.

> If anyone is in Christ, the new creation has come.
> The old has gone, the new is here! (2 Corinthians 5:17).

I had always read this Scripture about being a new creation, applying it to my personal spiritual identity as God's daughter at salvation. But it dawned on me at this very moment with Doug and Carol that the new creation God is forming through you and me is also our spiritual family. God is using the richness and diversity of all our human stories—through the sorrows, joys, wisdom gained, mistakes learned from, wounding, hurts, betrayals, traditions, and dreams—to heal us of loneliness, showing that what we have in common connects us to one another like a beautiful tapestry.

God's family is diverse, weaving together different cultures, families, and backgrounds, so we can see God healing us. So we can know God can really love us through the impossible, when friends who are closer than a brother become family.

• • •

I didn't have a watch with me in the bathroom, but as the hours ticked by, I got tired of sitting on the toilet seat waiting for Ah-Ma's anger to abate. I stepped into the tub and tried to see if I could lie down and sleep, like they do in the movies. It didn't work. I was very uncomfortable.

As I put my ear to the door and heard quiet for a very long time, I looked down through the gap at the bottom of the door to see if I could observe any shadows moving.

I slowly cracked open the door to see if the coast was clear. Gingerly, I tiptoed my way to my bedroom and locked the door. It was nearly 5 a.m. The sun would soon be up. I had not slept a wink.

Afraid my mother would swoop in any minute, I quickly folded some clothes—whatever I could find that wasn't shredded—put them in my bag along with my makeup kit, and threw in a few pairs of shoes. I got dressed, quietly grabbed my purse and keys, and closed the door behind me. I took the elevator to the ground floor and got in my car.

I closed my eyes to rest and pray. Cry. Then rest some more.

As the morning light rose, I put on my makeup using the rearview mirror and brushed my hair.

Then, at 8:30, I grabbed my bags and walked over to the front door of my apartment building to stand outside and wait. I waved Eric hello when he drove up in his indigo blue Camaro. He walked out to meet me, gave me a hug, took my bags, popped open the trunk, and opened the passenger door for me to climb in.

"Good morning!" Eric beamed. "Ready for a fun road trip?"

"Yes. Let's go!" I answered, no longer sure about anything, trying to forget about everything, so I could be at my best and not ruin my chances for love to stay.

God sets the lonely in families (Psalm 68:6).

LETTER TO MY YOUNGER SELF
You Are Worthy of Family

Beloved,

You were never meant to carry secrets alone indefinitely.

This burden of an untold story is too heavy for you to bear. You were created to share your burdens and feel connected to others deeply. You were created to live in the light, not to hide.

Family isn't created only by blood. True family is more than skin deep. True family is created by the Holy Spirit when you allow someone to step into your pain, letting them love you and lift you up.

When you allow someone to see where pain once wounded you, you discover that pain has purpose. You can offer your healing presence to encourage someone with your story. When you welcome and accept others—just as they are, not as they should be—there is beauty. There is no more loneliness, because there, in your broken, beautiful story, is God's love.

CHINESE NEW YEAR'S EVE REUNION DINNER

The Chinese New Year's Eve Reunion Dinner happens on the Lunar New Year's Eve as one of the most important meals for family members to eat together, with everyone traveling from no matter where they are to gather together. The dinner symbolizes starting a new year of hope and prosperity, leaving the sorrows of the past behind. A delicious feast of multiple dishes with symbolic meaning is enjoyed to bless everyone. It's like Thanksgiving for Americans. The practice of the New Year's Eve Reunion Dinner has been dated as early as the Northern and Southern Dynasty (AD 420–589) in China.

Being a part of a family is key to accessing this good life. For God's people, our blessing is belonging to a spiritual family, as we encourage each other, weeping with those who weep, rejoicing with those who rejoice. Because we have each other as God's family, we are never alone in this world.

Reflect and Share

- *What would you tell your younger self about keeping secrets and hiding shame?*

- *How is God guiding you to redefine family for yourself? Is God prompting you to confide in someone, freeing yourself from carrying the burden of your secrets?*

- *What were the taboos or family codes you grew up with? Who is someone you turned to in order to share a secret? What did they say?*

Chapter 20

Normal

W hen we went on this fateful Fourth of July road trip, Eric and I
had been dating for less than two months.

We were still in the trial period of our relationship. It was like working the first three-month probationary period of a new job, where if
you prove that your skills, performance, and compatibility are a good
fit, you become eligible for the perks of a permanent position, like holiday parties, access to bagels and granola in the break room, and use of
the company gym.

So, I was still trying to put my best foot forward to keep our conversations and time together light, fun, and happy. Like the way I saw
in the rom-coms. I became the uncomplicated, cheerful Bonnie, who
looked like a girl I felt guys would want to date. The simple Bonnie
who experienced everything good in life. Who belonged.

I was avoiding any topics that might steer us into the topic of my
dysfunctional family. At this stage in our budding romance, we were
still in our honeymoon period, and I wanted to enjoy this phase as long
as possible. Until, as I assumed, affection would fizzle out.

I figured things weren't getting serious anyhow, and maybe this
might be one of those dating relationships more for fun, that didn't
have the mileage to go the distance. On paper, we weren't compatible

in life circumstances. He lived the simple life. No burdens or ties to any responsibilities other than for himself. But as far as I could see, I had to take care of my mom and sister indefinitely. So, this whole meeting Eric thing was rather inconvenient. He did not fit into my plan of living my life out in duty, serving my mother and family.

• • •

Back when Eric and I first started dating, one early Saturday morning as Ah-Ma and I were eating breakfast, my cell phone rang. No one usually calls me that early on the weekend. I tried to ignore it, but my phone kept ringing and showing Eric's name.

"You're not seriously dating him, are you?" Ah-Ma said. It wasn't a question. More of a directive. "He doesn't speak Chinese. I can't talk to him. How can that ever work? It can't."

"Mom, we're just friends." I was hoping that, over time, Ah-Ma would be happy for me, since I was single in my thirties. My biological clock was ticking.

"Westerners don't respect their parents," Ah-Ma explained. "They just say, 'I love you' but then go off, get married, buy their own houses, live the good life, drive their own cars, and leave their parents in the dust and don't visit them except for Thanksgiving or Christmas."

"Eric's really nice, caring, and kind," I said as I tried to persuade her. "He loves God. He has such a good heart. He's a good guy." I was scared to say, "He makes me happy."

"So what? There are plenty of nice guys who love God and have a good heart," she retorted. "Out of all the people in the world, why choose *him*? Unless you want to get rid of me! He's not Chinese. Your husband should be someone who cares about Ah-Ma too. What good is marriage if it's just all about the two of you? Marriage is more than just two people. It's family."

I didn't know what to say.

"How can we live together—I won't even know what you two are talking about!" Ah-Ma's arms shot out, gesticulating like she was cracking a whip in the air. "I didn't live this long to be some dumb, old lady cooking for the two of you. That's not family!"

"Who said we're getting married?" I exclaimed. "Ah-Ma, we're just friends!"

I was so certain Eric was the one, but now Ah-Ma made me doubt it all. That's the problem with being gaslighted. You don't realize it's happening. *What if I'm wrong?* Why cause trouble if this won't last, if he isn't "the one"? He didn't seem to fit to the job description anymore. And I was sure I didn't fit his either.

So I told myself to just keep it casual. Go down to Los Angeles and be carefree Bonnie. Leave messy Bonnie back home.

. . .

On the drive, Eric and I talked music, college days, and explored all possible conversation starters. But I avoided the topic of family for hours. Suddenly, Eric asked about my family.

Waterworks. Big time. My mascara was running.

"I'm not the girl you probably think I am," I said, deciding to burst his bubble. "My life is complicated. You don't want to get involved with me. You deserve to be with someone normal. I'm not normal. My family is not normal."

Eric was quiet for a minute. He reached for my hand. "I don't want normal. I'm interested in you. Tell me. What's going on?"

Oh, no! I thought. We're not even halfway to LA, and now it's all over. No more pixie dust. No more Simple Bonnie. I was Weird Bonnie now.

"If I tell you what my life is really like, I'm giving you permission— it's okay if you just want to be friends," I prefaced my talk. "My feelings won't be hurt. You didn't know what you were getting into."

"You can tell me," Eric said. "I want to know."

I could hardly navigate my own world with my own mother, especially after what happened the night before. There was no way I wanted to bring sweet Eric and drag him down into my crazy world. So, I figured it was best to turn him away by giving him the stone-cold truth for his own good. I gave him the whole nine yards, starting with what had happened the previous night. My mother threatening to commit suicide, how she cut up my clothes. It was awful—all the crying, my eyes swollen shut like Robert De Niro in *Raging Bull.*

As I blew my nose and an avalanche of tissue balls fell from my lap to the car floor, Eric reached for my hand.

"I guess I don't see the problem here," Eric protested. "*You're* the one I want to be with. Not your mother." And for some reason, this was funny to me. Because I started laughing between the tears.

"That's the problem," I said. "My mother expects to live with me and whoever I marry." There—I said it—blowing out any embers left to the flame of romance between us.

Eric chose his next words cautiously. "Would *you* want to live with your mom after you got married?"

Ah. God knew who He needed to send me. Somehow, somewhere in this big, wide world, God brought someone who carried the clarity of innocence combined with wisdom and discernment that comes from a kindred spirit who could see inside my heart.

I was quiet. And Eric gripped my hand tighter.

And my heart was taken captive by something new. I didn't recognize this feeling because I had never felt it before.

I thought it was curiosity, bewilderment, intrigue, and maybe confusion mixed with amazement. I thought the honeymoon part of our story was fading. But one moment of honesty became intimacy. What I did not recognize was God's love sparked in the heart of Eric and me. I was falling in love.

I could be flawed yet still loved. I could share my loneliness with someone who understood it. Who did not step away, but stepped closer to me. He had looked deep into my heart and, instead of leaving, he chose to stay.

But here was the problem: We were driving hundreds of miles away from my reality. Would I be jolted awake from this dream when I returned?

> The LORD does not look at the things people look at. People look at the outward appearance, but the LORD looks at the heart (1 Samuel 16:7).

LETTER TO MY YOUNGER SELF
You Are Worth Seeing

Beloved,

You fit. You belong. You're okay.

Your flaws don't disqualify you from being loved. Your flaws give someone access to really know and see you in your humanity. Your flaws give others permission to be themselves and know they belong. They are okay too.

Don't edit yourself. Because when you try to please everyone, you end up losing yourself. How can you let others get to know you if you can't be honest about who you are and who you aren't? How can you experience intimacy if you don't draw close enough to let someone else in?

You are your own kind of beautiful when you step into your vulnerable places. You are worth seeing.

MOSAIC ART

Making a mosaic involves the meticulous process of creating an artistic pattern or image by placing small, broken pieces of glass, ceramic, or shells of varying colors and sizes close together to cover a surface. Even though it is a 4,000-year-old craft in art history—seen across Greek, Roman, and Byzantine cultures as artisans decorated temples, palaces, and churches—the earliest known mosaics were Chinese.

When set together, the broken pieces create a paint-like effect because as different colors fuse together, they create shadows and a sense of depth. When a mosaic is made of glass, it shimmers and sparkles as dazzling light reflects off the surface.

Mosaics are created by placing broken pieces that might appear flawed but, in fact, create beautiful art! What a brilliant image of what happens when we willingly set out the seemingly odd-shaped pieces of our lives that don't fit any category, and we share transparently in community. How much more attractive we would be as a community of faith to each other if we could be real and show that we do not all lead the same cookie-cutter lives! We are all unfinished works of art. Everyone will feel they have a place where they can belong when they see a rich variety of differences being celebrated, valued, and accepted, rather than everyone being forced into a monochrome mold, where there are outsiders and insiders.

In the hands of our Master Artist, we are placed alongside each other not to fix each other, but to simply celebrate our lives just as they are—to represent the different colors of life. God fuses us together to create shadows and depth. He is involved in every detail of our lives, walking with us no matter what our color, failure, tragedy, type of family, economic status, age, or health situation happens to be. Our most intense moments of pain, anxiety, struggles, and joy are not wasted when it comes to this holy art. The picture of Christ cannot glitter without every piece of your human experience.

You are the gift that glitters. You are worthy to shine. You are worthy to be you.

Reflect and Share

- *What would you tell your younger self about embracing her flaws?*

- *How is God guiding you to be more honest about what you've been through?*

- *How do you define a "normal" person or a "normal" life? What events inspired you to grow in self-acceptance?*

Chapter 21

Gift Basket

When Eric and I got back from Los Angeles, I didn't know what I would find walking into my apartment. We first looked in the parking garage to see if we could spy Ah-Ma's car. It was still parked there. I exhaled. *Okay. No dead body there. Ah-Ma is home.*

My fingers were frozen cold from anxiety, like I was stepping through a fog as I climbed up the stairwell, headed down the hall, turned the keys, and opened the door slowly.

Ah-Ma was sitting on the living room couch, watching TV. Ah-Ma was alive.

I was relieved. Then, I was scared. *What do I say to her?*

"Ah-Ma, I'm home," I tried to say nonchalantly, as I walked through to the bedroom.

Ah-Ma got up without saying a word, walked to her bedroom, and slammed the door. I slept with the door locked every night, beginning that day forward.

To be honest, I don't have very many memories of home life since that road trip. I'm sure my nervous system blocked them out and, one day, when God knows I'm ready, I'll have to deal with those memories. For now, God has chosen to keep them locked away.

What I do know is that I eventually could not handle living in fear of my well-being after that road trip. I was having trouble sleeping, and it was affecting me. I was confiding in Carol regularly now, and she had an idea. "Is there someone you can stay with for a while? Just so you can catch your breath? It's not good to live in fear all the time."

That's when Sally—an older, wise, and loving woman who is beloved among our church community—popped to my mind. Sally is beautiful inside and out. She looks like Ava Gardner—the kind of woman who exudes classic beauty, like she could have appeared on the cover of *Time* magazine. But she's also the kind of friend who will invite you to fold your feet up on her sofa and curl up in conversation together over a mug of tea, after she hugs you like you're her long-lost niece, welcoming you in the door. Her home reflects her love of flowers, and there is always a pot of tea ready to pour, along with a listening ear and a peculiar gift for asking the kind of questions that connect the dots in your stories, encouraging your heart after each visit.

Sally lives in a really nice part of town, with a garden bigger than the house, and a rose garden planted near a grove of trees. Sally and her husband, Mike, share the gift of hospitality generously by opening their home all the time, hosting church group events. In particular, she offered to let over a hundred of our thirtysomething singles host our potlucks there. When my mother was sick, and I was in need of a place to stay while I helped Ah-Ma seek medical treatment in Arizona, Sally graciously offered use of her family cabin, without any payment.

"We are God's family," Sally said. I didn't even know Sally when she offered me the use of her cabin by the river. Pastor Rich mentioned Sally had a place near where Ah-Ma needed treatment, and I reached out to inquire about cost.

Sally shocked me by saying, "You are welcome to use it. Just let me know the dates."

So when I was searching my mind for someone whom I could ask to stay with, I thought of Sally. But look: It's one thing to use someone's vacation cabin. It's entirely another thing to invite yourself to live in someone's home with their family!

I didn't have anything really to offer Sally in return. It's not like I was anyone important, with special connections or status. What reason would I give for needing a place to stay? *Excuse me, but my mom is unstable, and I'm afraid she might kill me, so can I come live with you and Mike, sleep in your guest room, and basically be your housemate?*

"Well, it doesn't hurt to ask," Carol offered.

So, I took another step of faith, testing to see how far God might provide a new way for me, like Gideon putting out a fleece to see if it would be wet or dry.

"Here's a strange favor I wanted to ask," I began to say to Sally. It was hard to ask someone such a big, unusual favor. I was always afraid of being pitied, but I was learning that needing help isn't weakness. Asking for help was a sign I was beginning to believe I was worthy of friendship, love, and care. Expressing my need to another trusted person signified I believe that God's family isn't just a theory, but a reality.

I told Sally a gentle version of the truth, that I started dating someone, and my mother wasn't taking it well. That there was conflict between us, and I was scared for my well-being because of her anger issues. And I needed to find a safe place to stay for a while. "Would you and Mike be willing to let me use one of your guest rooms for a bit?" Gosh, it felt so embarrassing. I was grimacing on the phone as I asked, heart beating, my whole body flushed and sweating.

I quickly added, "And no worries at all if that isn't something you and Mike can do." I didn't want to put Sally on the spot. "This is your home, so I understand the guest room might be reserved for family or close friends." More cringing on my part as I held my breath.

"I'm so sorry this is so hard for you and your mother, Bonnie. That sounds heartbreaking. You love your mother so much." Sally's words flowed like a balm to my heart. "Let me talk with Mike and get back with you. I just need to make sure the calendar is free."

Thank You, Jesus, I whispered, hanging up, relieved, and with tears of joy and amazement. God's family was really real. There was a loving world beyond the walls of fear and isolation.

For the first time, I was leaving home. Not just in my body, because I had lived in the dorms and with roommates in college. But I was leaving home as the little girl in my heart, in search of the woman God had created me to grow into becoming.

· · ·

I stayed with Sally and Mike for many months. In the evenings, Sally and Mike graciously set a place for me at the table, and it was like winning a Willy Wonka golden ticket being a part of their lives. Living in a peaceful home was not only possible, but it was joyful to see Sally and Mike relate to each other as friends, even like newlyweds, after decades of marriage.

It wasn't just superficial talk, but they showed genuine care and interest about my life and the things that turned my world as well as my heart. They shared their own life stories and offered me wise counsel without giving me advice about my situation. They prayed with me, seeking God's guidance in what lay ahead.

After some time, I didn't want to wear out my welcome, so I made plans to return home. I actually didn't know my next steps, but I wanted to get out from the control of Ah-Ma and live in emotional safety. So when Eric came to pick me up, load up my luggage, and carry it up to my apartment, I was despondent. I didn't want to live in fear anymore, feeling anxious over what lay ahead of me.

"Let's go take a drive," Eric suggested. "We'll come back later."

As we got back in the car, I thought we'd head to a café and grab a cup a coffee and some pastry.

"Why don't we go to the beach?" Eric said. "You like the beach."

I love the beach. It gives me so much peace to be there. But it was about to rain.

"No, I'll be okay. We don't have to go to the beach," I insisted. "Look at the dark clouds. A storm is coming. It's gonna rain really bad."

"That's okay. It's probably intermittent," Eric replied. "Just a little rain."

I knew Eric wanted to cheer me up, but I didn't want him to drive all the way to San Francisco, to Ocean Beach, only to sit in the car because it was raining. Ocean Beach is my favorite beach because the sand there is fine, the stretch of land next to the sea is wide and flat, and the water breaking onto the shore extends for miles and miles. This is a good beach for walking in quietness, watching lemmings skedaddle across the surf. But it was cold, and I wasn't in the mood to be outside.

I was too tired to protest, but the further north we drove, the more violently the rain came down. We were hydroplaning as buckets of water dumped on us, the windshield wipers swish-swashing maniacally, I could have sworn they were going to fly off. *Splash!* The wind was whipping up water sideways across the freeway, blowing so fiercely that we could feel the car starting to drift if Eric didn't grip the steering wheel hard enough to right the car after each gust blew through.

"Eric," I calmly stated, while clutching the car grab handle above me. "It's okay. *Really*. It's raining cats and dogs. Let's go to the beach another day."

"We're fine! We're almost there," Eric replied.

As we pulled into a parking spot on the street off Taraval across from Ocean Beach, the rain stopped falling. "I can't believe it!" I smiled. "We can go outside! Hurry! Before it starts raining again!"

We scrambled out of the car and hurriedly put our coats on, like astronauts suiting up to enter outer space, pulling gloves onto our hands, and adding scarves, hats, and as many layers as we could pack on. We ran across the street hand in hand as the wind whipped around us.

We climbed over the grass tundra and stepped onto the beach. Absolutely no one else was there. We were the first to step onto the virgin shore, made smooth by the waves that had pounded up onto the sand. We walked like space people on the moon, the entire stretch of land before us an otherworldly, glassy surface.

We stared at each other with looks of astonishment, mouths open in bewilderment, then smiling from ear to ear. "There's no one here but us!" Eric yelled into the wind. It was so loud we could hardly hear each other.

"It's so beautiful! Look!" I replied, reaching down into the soggy sand, saturated with seawater. "It's a sand dollar!"

All around us, for stretches of miles as far as the eye could see, the beach was dotted with sand dollars washing up en masse after the storm that had just blown through. The clouds were dark, and the shore looked like the surface of the moon. We stepped out onto the wind-swept beach and noticed, one after another, sand dollars battered by the waves, hiding in the sand.

We ran like kids on a treasure hunt, digging them up. Among the specks of white poking out of the sand, many were broken. But among the broken pieces, we found whole sand dollars hidden on the shore. We put them in our pockets.

By the time we stopped because our sandy fingers and noses were frozen cold, our pockets were bulging full of sand dollars. As we made our way back toward the hill to return to our car, the sun suddenly broke through the dark clouds, sending a golden stream of sunlight across the beach.

"Look, Eric! The sand…" I cried, pointing to the sand dune suddenly bathed in the brilliance of the sun. "The sand—it's sparkling like diamonds!"

Instead of answering me, Eric said, "Sit down here."

There was a nearby large drift log on the beach from a tree washed up by the storm. He was taking off his backpack, rummaging in the pockets. I figured it was snack time, but then Eric got down on one knee, opened up a box with a ring, and asked me the question I never had imagined was possible less than year ago.

"I love you, Bonnie. Would you do me the honor? Will you marry me?"

Brokenness no longer meant loneliness. My heart, like the sand dollars on Ocean Beach, was full of broken pieces, and yet here, God was bringing me a wholeness newly discovered. I am both. Brokenness and wholeness both exist, held together by God's love. God's love, big like the ocean, fathomlessly and mysteriously deep enough, carried both brokenness and beauty. Somehow, in this big, lonely, broken world, God had brought someone into my life to take my hand and to become the living expression of that love, so we could grow into this broken, beautiful life together, as husband and wife. This was the moment I said yes.

• • •

I called Sally to share the good news and asked her if I could stay with her and Mike until my wedding day. I was too afraid to live at home with Ah-Ma now that I was engaged. Sally said yes, and Eric drove me back to Sally's that same day.

I stood at a crossroads in my life. I once promised Ah-Ma that I would take care of her my whole life. But I couldn't walk away from Eric. Love wouldn't let me go.

Was I destined to only be the daughter of my mother, or would I step into my identity as the daughter of my Heavenly Father—free to choose her path, to be loved? What would this life look like if I dared to be Eric's beloved?

When I was a little girl, all I wanted to do was to make my mom proud. To make her happy. She was the sun, and my heart orbited around her. But God was opening my heart to see that the mother I wanted, the mother I tried to love into being, didn't exist. It was time to accept the reality of the toxic mother I had. I had to grieve the death of my expectations and dreams for the ideal mom I longed for, so I could grow into the daughter of a loving Heavenly Father.

Jesus said, "Then you will know the truth, and the truth will set you free" (John 8:32). It's important to God that we trust Him with the truth, even if it hurts. We experience an intimate rest when we give God the burdens we were never meant to carry. We can begin to make different choices that are healthy for ourselves, our spouses, and our children, and break hurtful, old patterns. We stop becoming enablers for hurtful people in our lives whom we love, so they can face the truth of their brokenness with God too. Even as we honor our parents, we are not to take responsibility for their faults or brokenness. I began learning about breaking codependency and creating boundaries, delineating where others' control over us ends and our self-control, a fruit of the Holy Spirit, begins.

People sometimes ask me if I've forgiven my mother. I have done the hard work of grieving and healing. I have forgiven my mother. She was my whole life, and I love her more than anyone may know. But while forgiveness takes one person, reconciliation takes two. Honoring our parents does not mean open borders to toxicity, fear, intimidation, or manipulation.

In order to step into my new beginning with Eric, there would be a leaving of an old, dysfunctional, and toxic life. There was no going back. Ah-Ma would make good on her promise to leave me.

"You made your choice," Ah-Ma said when I told her I was getting married and would not continue to live with her as I began my new life with Eric. She would eventually move in with other family members after I got married.

I wanted my mother to be happy for us, so I went to Chinatown to buy traditional gifts—dried abalone, scallops, lotus roots, Chinese bird's nest, cakes, bakery goods—to make a traditional wedding basket usually given by the groom's family to the mother of the bride. In the Western tradition, engagement gifts are exchanged between the bride and groom. But in the Chinese tradition, gifts are exchanged between the bride's and groom's families. I gave the gifts to her on behalf of both Eric and myself. I didn't know much about this tradition, so I customized my own basket with things I knew my mother liked and found valuable. They were symbolic of hope that Ah-Ma would reciprocate her blessing and goodwill. Honestly, it was more of a peace offering.

"Oh, just a few gifts. So easy for you to get rid of me," Ah-Ma said. Ever since I was young, Ah-Ma had said I should never forget to be a good daughter when I chose a husband. That we should live together. "If he really wants to just live with the two of you, then you both should buy me a house. Your happiness doesn't have anything to do with me. Calling me Ah-Ma is pointless. It doesn't mean anything anymore."

I had made my choice, and it would soon become official. I would live with my choice to become Bonnie Gray 'til death do us part.

> Let the beloved of the LORD rest secure in him, for he shields him all day long, and the one the LORD loves rests between his shoulders (Deuteronomy 33:12).

LETTER TO MY YOUNGER SELF
You Are Worthy of Rest and Self-Care

Beloved,

Everything beautiful in nature moves by God's invitation in quietness and rest,

You are no less. Start believing you are worthy of feeding your soul. Prioritize your well-being.

It is not easy for you to see where you begin and others end. You'd rather burn out than disappoint others. But you'll need strength for the journey, so get away to rest awhile. Get refreshed and refilled. You'll need to take radical steps to practice healthy boundaries.

Ask others to help you. You'll be surprised by the many kind and generous people who understand and are walking this journey of rest, and you'll become one of them too.

BIRD'S NEST SOUP

Edible bird nests are a prized Chinese delicacy. The bird nests are made out of the sticky saliva from swiftlets found in caves and cliffs and are harvested entirely for human consumption. Because it is very dangerous to climb up to caves for harvesting the nests, and because the nests are built by the birds only a few times a year, nests are sold at prices up to $3,000 per pound. The nests are high in minerals like calcium, magnesium, and potassium, and when dissolved in broth, they are believed to enhance one's health and immune system.[1]

It's the promise of rest, revitalizing body and soul, and the rarity of such a dish that bring so many to value its worth. The gift of life and vitality is what we all long for, which God's love restores in us.

—————————— **Reflect and Share** ——————————

- *What would you tell your younger self about the importance of taking time and making space for rest and self-care?*

- *How is God guiding you to be more aware of your need for emotional and physical rest?*

- *What was a time in your life that led you to make significant changes in your schedule, your routine, or your relationships to prioritize your well-being? Did anyone come alongside you to support you?*

Chapter 22

Double Happiness

W hen I was engaged, everyone was happy on Eric's side. His family was ecstatic for us. Eric's dad, Butch, talked to me on the
phone after Eric called home with the good news. He said, "This is
great news! Now Eric won't be alone."

Usually, when an engagement is announced, there are hearty congratulations, friends want to see your ring, and everyone starts asking
you "When's the big day?" and "Do you know what you want your
wedding dress to look like?" It's all fun, dreaming up your special day.

It was not that way for me as a Chinese bride. This was a side of the
engagement that Eric didn't know about because he wasn't Chinese. As
a Chinese daughter, my engagement came with a lot of expectations I
could not fulfill.

Ah-Ma expected a betrothal gift. In Chinese tradition, a betrothal
gift is a symbolic amount of money showing the groom's family's gratitude to the bride's parents for raising her up. It happens during the
engagement as a way the bride's family agrees to let their daughter go,
since they were the ones to bear the expense and hard work of raising
a good daughter. Since I was going to be "transferred" into my in-law's
family, taking on the groom's name and carrying on the groom's line

and future generations, I would no longer be considered part of my mother's side of the family. So this Chinese wedding tradition, *pin jin*, is a bride price symbolizing the groom's family's respect. The amount of money the groom gives symbolizes the bride's value to the groom's family. This is a very old-fashioned, outdated tradition that wasn't practiced at all in my generation. I knew of no Chinese American friends in my circles who did this.

However, in my case, ever since I was a little girl, Ah-Ma had said she would only agree to letting me live with my husband if we were willing to buy her a home with a deed written to her in her name. Otherwise, Ah-Ma expected to live with us right from the beginning, as matriarch of our family, and I would continue to cover all her living and discretionary expenses. "I'm not going to give away my daughter for nothing!"

Needless to say, I hoped this was just Ah-Ma negotiating high—maybe more symbolic than reality. But as my relationship with my mother broke apart because I could not fulfill Ah-Ma's demands, I began to separate myself from my Chinese identity. Ah-Ma was irrevocably tied to my Chinese self. It was too painful for me to listen to Chinese music, speak Chinese, or even go in Chinese grocery stores.

My heart was broken and, like the scene of a fatal car crash, I could not go near the cultural epicenter where my Chinese self was born: Chinatown. All I could think of was Ah-Ma whenever I thought of Chinatown, as I bore the shame and pain of not having a mother during a time that should have been one of the most exciting times for a bride and her mother.

One of the wedding traditions I had always looked forward to when I was little girl, as I imagined getting married, was wearing the traditional Chinese red silk wedding dress called a cheongsam that Ah-Ma would embroider. Just like the white wedding dress is reserved only for the blushing bride in the Western world, the red cheongsam or silk dress is reserved only for the lucky bride.

The jewelry I would wear with my red cheongsam on my wedding day would be given to me by my mother, representing that I was loved and valued. I soaked this message in because whenever Ah-Ma and I attended any family or friend's wedding banquet, Ah-Ma would point to the bride, who wore layers and layers of solid-gold necklaces, pendants, and bracelets. Sometimes, the bride wore so many bangle bracelets that they would go up to her elbows. "Look," Ah-Ma pointed out. "All that gold means she is valuable to her family. She's worth a lot to her parents and worth a lot to the groom's family too."

Once in a while, when I was a kid, whenever a family friend's daughter was getting married, and the wedding drew near, Ah-Ma took me jewelry shopping in Chinatown. We'd stand outside the glass doors of the jewelry store to get buzzed in by the owner. You knew you were in a fancy place because you couldn't just walk in off the street. The store owner would take the 24 karat gold necklace Ah-Ma had pointed out in the glass display, put it on a scale to weigh it, pull out his plastic calculator, punch in the cost of gold for that day, multiply the price by the weight, and show Ah-Ma the number. I would always be in awe of how much cash Ah-Ma dropped, spreading hundred-dollar bills out on the glass counter, when we were always such spendthrifts. I didn't even know she had that kind of money stashed somewhere. But, of course, I didn't say a thing.

So, just like brides in Western culture squeal with oohs and aahs when their mom, sister, or friend gives them "something blue" to represent pure love, a Chinese bride beams and knows she is of high value when she gets "something 24 karat gold." A Chinese bride who is beloved might also wear a special piece of jade—a jade pendant or bracelet given by the women in her family. One time, Ah-Ma and I were saying congratulations at the end of a wedding reception line. Ah-Ma complimented the bride on how beautiful her large jade jewelry pendant was. The bride proudly told us that her grandmother had passed it to her—an heirloom to bless her with good health and lots of babies.

I secretly believed that when the day came, Ah-Ma would pass down one of the pieces of jade I had seen in her jewelry box.

A third gift I would be happy to receive as a Chinese bride was a double red envelope filled with a monetary gift to represent double happiness. It's not the amount of money that matters, but it's symbolic of your family's blessings for you as a new couple. When a woman is single, she gets one red envelope at Chinese New Year, but when she gets married, she will receive two—one for her and another for her husband.

I loved all these beautiful rites of passage and longed for them. These gifts meant you were a cherished, proper, respectable daughter and honored bride. These gifts said you were a daughter of high value, greatly prized. These gifts would signify you were loved and came from a good family.

So, even though I knew that Ah-Ma had cut me off, and even though the day before the wedding, I still did not know if she would attend, I hoped for her to somehow have a change of heart and give some token of her blessing.

I felt Ah-Ma's pain, and I understood why she felt I had betrayed her. Ah-Ma was born and raised in a different culture than mine. But, in my heart of hearts, I hoped for a Hallmark movie ending on my wedding day. I hoped Ah-Ma was still thinking of me, that she wouldn't leave me barren of honor on my wedding day.

● ● ●

I had asked Ah-Ma to light my bride's candle during the wedding ceremony, alongside Eric's mother, who would light the groom's candle. But she refused. "That's what you get for trying to look respectable in front of your friends. You don't respect me. Why should I light some stupid candle for show? Forget about it. It's not happening. I'm not even going to be there. Then everyone will see what a dishonorable daughter you are. Your own mother won't even attend."

My soul was crushed. How could Eric and I symbolically light our unity candle if I eliminated the portion of the ceremony with our mothers? As I shared this latest potential change in the wedding service with Carol, she said, "I would be honored to light your candle, if she doesn't want to light it."

Since I did not have a father, I called Pastor Rich to ask him if he would do me the honor of giving me away. Rich replied, "I would be honored. When and where? I'll be there!"

As I walked down the aisle with my arm holding fast to the strong, sturdy arm of Rich, I saw my bride's candle lit by Carol, glimmering on the communion table. I saw my beloved Eric, standing tall and handsome in black tux and white bow tie, with tears in his eyes and love in his heart, gazing into my soul and my whole being. I wore a long, cathedral train veil, flowing over a strapless, white satin wedding gown and pearl earrings I had picked out to match the silver in the embroidered bodice.

To adorn my neck, arms, or body, there was nothing borrowed or blue—just a string of freshwater pearls that were newly handmade, lovingly crafted and beaded by Sally, fastened together by a silver clasp. On the morning of my wedding, Sally left the necklace in a jewelry box for me at the dining table, with a note on it. "To Bonnie. With all my love, Sally."

For our church wedding ceremony, I wore my Western-style wedding gown. But that night, I changed into the traditional Chinese, one-piece, red silk cheongsam (*quipao*) wedding dress. As I wore the color red to signify happiness, good luck, and prosperity in my new life as the bride, Eric and I toasted our guests at our Chinese wedding banquet, which is the Chinese tradition, where the new couple goes to each table to toast their family and friends. Newlyweds offer the toast as a sign of deep respect and sincere gratitude for those attending their celebration. The toasting happens right before dessert, at the end of a multicourse meal. It symbolized to me that life is only sweet because of the family and friends that are there to share in life's joys and celebrations. We are only rich because of the people who love us and fill our lives with the blessing of their presence. This is what I deeply felt, as Eric and I made our way to each table to thank our friends and the people who had become my family, in every sense of the word.

I love you, I said, hugging my friends that night as we stood in the final reception goodbye line as husband and wife. I was wearing my firecracker-red Chinese wedding dress—my silk cheongsam that I had longed to wear as a little girl standing tippy toe in front of the hallway mirror in Chinatown. But instead of a peacock embroidered on my red dress, I chose peony flowers, because I whispered to my Abba Father, "I am Your beloved daughter." Like the flowers opening in blooms, as I stood there with my forever love Eric, I saw the true spiritual family God had blessed me with—the friends who loved me as their sister and friend.

My friends become family in my brokenness, and their worth is more than rubies. Even though I was not adorned with any gold necklaces or jade bracelets, even though I didn't hold double red envelopes in my hands that night, I was blossoming in double happiness. Because hand in hand with my new husband, we were now stepping into a new life as one. My heart was bursting with peace and joy because of God remaking my brokenness into beauty.

My Heavenly Father knew that the journey ahead for me to return to Chinatown had only just begun. He was making something new by bringing me back to the place where my story began. On such a happy day, I thought there was nothing for me back in Chinatown.

Like so many things I was unlearning, I would learn I was wrong.

> Behold, I am going to do something new, now it will spring up; will you not be aware of it? I will even make a roadway in the wilderness, rivers in the desert (Isaiah 43:19 NASB).

LETTER TO MY YOUNGER SELF
You Are Worthy of Happiness

Beloved,

Love will always find a way. You don't need to even be aware of it. Like the river quietly replenishing itself each spring, there is no place you can find yourself where Jesus will not go with you.

Lean into Jesus. He will make a way for you.

I know it is hard to believe so much happiness can be true for you. But not even doubt can take away what God has intended for you. Nothing is impossible for your Heavenly Father. He delights to see you blossom with happiness.

You are beautiful and beloved. God is making all things new in you.

DRAGON AND PHOENIX BANGLES

Since gold represents the highest value in Chinese culture, giving gold jewelry to the bride represents that she is a valued member of the family. Twenty-four karat gold jewelry pieces are usually worn by the bride only once—at her wedding—and are then placed in a safe-deposit box, to later be passed down to the next generation.

One important piece of wedding-day jewelry is a bangle intricately carved with the images of a dragon and a phoenix. The dragon represents the groom, and the phoenix represents the bride. These images symbolize strength and power in unity. When a bride wears them stacked along her wrists, it signifies that the new couple is blessed by their families to enjoy a harmonious marriage together. She is an honored woman.

Reflect and Share

- *What would you tell your younger self about what happiness looks like?*

- *How is God inspiring you to experience more happiness in your life today?*

- *If you are single, what is your vision of happiness? If you are married, what were the hard things about your wedding day, and what were the happy things?*

Chapter 23

Chinese Hospital

We finally arrived at 845 Jackson Street at the Chinese Hospital. Its red pagoda rooftop framing the entrance made it feel like I was stepping back in time to a different place. Today, if you go there, the original Chinese Hospital building I found that afternoon and was born in has been demolished to build a new, modern, box-like facility.

I understood new upgrades were needed, but now it looked like every other hospital. I wished they hadn't destroyed so much history and cultural significance. Gone were the beautiful eastern architectural design flourishes, like the green tiles decorating the eaves. Gone was the name of the hospital inscribed in Chinese calligraphy, painted in gold above a traditional Asian arch gateway.

Curiously enough, I was returning here to find the little girl I had abandoned once I became a bride and was soon—within a year—pregnant with my first baby. I gave birth to Josh right as I turned 35. As I fell off planet Earth into the mysterious black hole of motherhood: being a stay-at-home mom, playing with Little People figurines, living the treadmill life of naps, snacks, and park playdates, ripping up little pieces of paper for Josh to use as "play garbage" to put into his toy garbage truck, I became pregnant with my second baby boy, Caleb.

As any mom of two little people three years old and under knows, a few hours of preschool—time to be with just the baby while the older child is playing with Play-Doh—can make the critical difference between sanity and a Jekyll-and-Hyde level of cray cray. I needed to enroll Josh in summer school, so I went searching for his birth certificate, and that's how I stumbled on my own forgotten birth certificate. As I stared at the document, my father's name, Kam Lee, wouldn't leave me. The word *Lee* was a constant reminder that my father was missing from my life. I carried the name of someone who had deserted me, without saying goodbye one last time.

After I married, I considered throwing out my maiden name to shed this painful identity of being abandoned. I eagerly embraced changing my last name. But something in me wanted to preserve the three letters *L-e-e*, like leaving the clothing label affixed to your shirt to identify the manufacturer, rather than ruining your shirt trying to tear it off (or if you do manage to cut it off, the remaining stubs scratch your neck like heck each time you move). I removed Sook-Wah as my middle name because other than my great-grandfather in China, no one ever called me by that name, and made Lee my middle name.

When I asked Ah-Ma why she chose my first name, Ah-Ma said the nurse needed her to pick a name to put on the birth certificate. So, my mother asked the nurse to read off English names from a baby book since she couldn't. Ah-Ma said *Bonnie* was the first name the nurse rattled off that felt easy for her to holler out, to call me to come to her. That's how I was named.

The only time I was called by a name in Chinese, it wasn't even my real name. When Ah-Ma finally gained U.S. citizenship, able to fulfill her promise to emigrate her family to America, my mother told me I would be called by a new name. I was five years old when my grandma Po-Po, grandpa Gung-Gung, and my five aunts and uncles immigrated to the U.S., and we all lived together under one roof. That was the same year my baby sister was born, and my parents separated.

"Your name is Man-Lei now," Ah-Ma instructed me. "So, when Po-Po and Gung-Gung come, they will call you Man-Lei. Don't tell them you are Sook-Wah. Understand?"

"Why?" I was confused.

"You don't have to know why," Ah-Ma answered abruptly. "Your grandma once had a daughter who died named Sook-Yin. So you can't be called Sook-Anything. You'll remind everyone of her dead baby."

"But who is Man-Lei? What does it mean?" I asked.

"Man-Lei is a famous Hong Kong actress," my mother replied. "You're lucky I chose that name for you, okay? Don't ask me any more questions."

"Okay," I replied.

. . .

I always thought it was odd that my father left us right after Ah-Ma's family immigrated. Later, when I grew up and read about Chinese American history, I learned how the Chinese Exclusion Act gave birth to creative ways of gaining entry to the land of opportunity that was open to European immigrants but denied to people of Chinese descent. I learned about paper wives—women in China who agreed to arranged marriages with fake identity papers that would let them enter the U.S. I secretly wondered if my mom's marriage echoed this story line.

I never gave it more than a quick thought. Who cares what happened in the past? What's important is the future I'm creating now, right? Doesn't the Bible say the old has passed, and we are a new creation anyway? Sounded good to me.

But when I arrived on the doorstep of the Chinese Hospital and touched its walls, I suddenly felt the enormity of the physical presence of this hospital. This building was old. It stood here as our country fell on its knees during the Great Depression. The clanging hand trucks delivering the pallets of bok choy by laborers hollering to each other across the street were real. Words bellowed out in Toi-San and Cantonese—the prominent Chinese dialects spoken by locals like my father and his family—ricocheting around me were not foreign, but familiar in the way the phrase *biscuits and gravy* voiced in a Southern drawl means home to so many.

Having not heard Chinese spoken for so many years, I started to cry, because the little girl in me recognized my native tongue, hearing the singsong dialects she had spoken daily.

I stood there as aging seniors passed by, and tired moms pulling their metal shopping carts filled with the day's groceries hurried their little ones, and grandmas pulled along rosy-cheeked toddlers by the hand. Pride swelled in me. All these little boys and girls were growing up into their stories, and because this was America, there was no telling where their journeys would lead.

As I looked up at the aging walls of the hospital that had stood there since 1925, I imagined the thousands of new mothers stepping through its doors. I thought of all the Chinese American girls enslaved in the sex trade in Chinatown during the nineteenth century—girls whose corpses, prior to the hospital being built, were thrown out in the alley because medical care was missing. The first Chinese people were forced to stay isolated in Chinatown, without access to schools and hospitals that were open to the rest of San Franciscans. It was only later, at the turn of the century, that Western medicine and care was provided through the Tung Wah Dispensary, staffed by Christian missionaries. After the 1906 earthquake destroyed the dispensary, the hospital was built.[1]

I suddenly saw the miracle of being born in this little hospital that began with people of faith, by missionaries in America. I was here, and this was the gateway through which I was carried as a little bundle out into the world.

The little Chinatown girl was still me. I may have been born to a mail-order bride, but God is the author of my story. I felt a newfound conviction: I had a right to know how my story began.

I looked at my birth certificate. I had two parents, not just one.

I need to find my father. Where is Kam Lee?

* * *

I couldn't sleep that night. *What if he's dead already?*

I slipped out of bed. Trying hard to not wake Eric up, I tiptoed downstairs, popped open my laptop, and typed his name in the search bar. In a matter of seconds, only three names popped up for northern California. One person was located just 20 minutes from where I lived. I couldn't believe it. There he was, in the online white pages.

How could this be? Was my father staring at the moon at the same time as me, driving down the same freeways all these decades?

The next day, I went where no one would disturb me. I closed the door to my bathroom and dialed.

"Ha-low!" an old man's voice hollered.

"Hi, is this Kam Lee? This is Bonnie. Your daughter." I said this in English, like I was announcing my name on a conference call at work. I couldn't bring myself to say *Dad* or *Bah-Ba*.

"What you want?" he blared back. This was not the greeting I imagined for our first exchange. I realized he might be worried that I wanted money. Maybe he thought I was still poor.

"I'm grown up now. I'm graduated from college. Married with two boys. A stay-at-home mom." I was rattling off my résumé. I switched to speaking Chinese because I wanted to be clear. "I'm not looking for anything. I called because I wanted to ask if I can come see you."

"Okay," he said. We politely shared contact numbers like drivers awkwardly exchanging insurance information at the scene of an accident.

Date and time were set. In less than a ten-minute call, I had invited myself to visit a man who had left me standing in a broken driveway as a little girl, bawling my eyes out as he drove away in his olive-green Nova over 30 years ago. I called him my daddy, and tomorrow I would see him again.

> You will be a crown of splendor in the Lord's hand, a royal diadem in the hand of your God (Isaiah 62:3).

LETTER TO MY YOUNGER SELF
Your History Is Worth Honoring

Beloved,

You've lived like you're a pauper, but your true identity is royalty. God not only knitted you with His love, but He also wove His purpose into your story.

Your soul is crowded by worries and cares. Loneliness was your middle name. But you've been adopted now. You've inherited a new name as God's beloved daughter.

Your history is worth honoring. It's the story of how you became His.

BRONZE VESSELS

Ancient China ushered in the era of the Bronze Age beginning around 2000 BC. During the Shang Dynasty, beautiful bronze vessels were crafted by artists.

A special method used was piece-mold casting—"sculpting" the metal by first creating a clay mold of the model, cutting it in sections, and reassembling it after the firing. The Metropolitan Museum of Art explains the benefit of this technique: "The decorative patterns could be carved or stamped directly on the inner surface of the model before it was fired. This technique enabled the bronze worker to achieve a high degree of definition in even the most intricate designs."[2]

When you look at individual pieces of your life, you might not see the purpose God inscribed into your life. But when they are all put together, you will see the beauty of His story carved into yours, having walked with you through the fire of life.

Reflect and Share

- *What would you tell your younger self about the importance of her history?*

- *How is God piquing your curiosity about your family history?*

- *What is an interesting bit of history trivia you know about your family? What is something you wish you knew about your family history?*

Chapter 24

The Bakery

Make a beeline to the bakery. If you don't get there early enough, everyone else will grab the thing you love, and you'll find yourself standing in front of an empty tray of crumbs. I'm talking about the Golden Gate Bakery on Grant Avenue.

There's always a long line, but once you step into the store, your heart palpitates with excitement, as workers in baker smocks stomp up the steps from the basement kitchen below, carrying heavy metal trays with oven mitts, yelling *"Don Tat!"* It means you'll soon be holding a piping hot egg tart in your hands, which you should immediately eat on the spot without delay. The flaky crust will melt in your mouth, as miraculously buttery as it is crispy. Any croissant in Paris would proudly call it its Asian sister.

By the time you've moved up the line snaking out the door, and it's your turn to order, you'll want to order enough pastries to fill a large pink box's worth of goodies. It would be a crime to leave without a box, right?

To order at a Chinese bakery, you can't be shy. Summon your courage, stand up straight, and holler very loudly for what you want because the places Chinese people inhabit are very *yeet lau* ("hotly festive"), which means people talk very loudly. So when you go in, get right up close to the glass countertop display and point emphatically at the yellow puffy pineapple bun, which is a chewy relative of Portuguese bread, baked with a sweet, crunchy crust topping (my childhood favorite). Old men hard of hearing will yell for *gai mae bao* ("roostertail buns," which are like a skinny version of the British hot cross buns). So, signal you want those too. Throw in a couple of coconut macaroons, and you'll have something delicious to savor days later with a cup of tea.

But there's one pastry I never took home with me. This pastry is the coconut-crème-filled Chinese éclair called *nai yau bau* ("milky bun"), sprinkled with toasted coconut shavings, that reminded me of the one person I had tried to forget. As a child, in the morning light I watched him sitting at the dining table and taking bites of nai yau bau in one hand while turning pages to read the newspaper with the other. I remember how he gave his paper a little shake and a tap in the middle once to fold it up, leaving a wake of coconut flakes on the table where he sat.

Flashbacks of this one person kept resurfacing after I made my trip to Chinatown. I didn't understand why these memories were randomly returning. Because this person had left me when I was seven and never came back.

Little did I know while standing there eating pastries with Eric that one day I would return to signal the clerk across the glass counter to put a Chinese coconut éclair into my pink box.

I never, ever would have guessed that I would take that pink box, put it in my trunk, drive across town, and present it to the man I once called Bah-Ba. My father.

● ● ●

I didn't want to go find my father. Why should I be the one to look for him? He never wrote or called. Not once. Sometimes, on my birthday, I would open the mailbox, hoping to find a mysterious card addressed to me from my daddy. But year after year, there was nothing.

Didn't he ever think about me? I thought he might be dead, but the child support checks kept coming in the mail.

The other theory I secretly harbored was that Ah-Ma was behind my MIA father. This was an unspeakable idea, but it was my last line of defense against the conclusion that my father just didn't love me.

Ah-Ma did not knit with yarn, but she intricately strung words around your soul so cruelly that your heart and mind became entangled in a web of confusion, no matter how hard you tried to please her. Nothing I ever did was enough. Her verbal assaults were like drive-by shootings—a flurry of attacks when I was innocently studying at my desk, lying on my bed, or standing over the sink and washing dishes.

Just like my Ah-Ma forbade me to see my father, could my mother have also prevented Bah-Ba from seeing me?

I held out hope until I turned 18. It was a little girl's fantasy tucked away in my heart. It played out like a scene from an after-school TV special, with my daddy showing up on my doorstep. It went something like this:

"You've finally turned 18! That's why Daddy's here. Your mom can't stop me from seeing you anymore!" Cue the tears. We both embrace. "I've always loved you. Ah-Ma must have taken all the letters I sent to you." More tears. Daddy and daughter cry over each other. Hugs and promises to make up for lost time are exchanged and proclaimed.

So, at my high school graduation ceremony, I scanned the crowd of family and friends mobbing my classmates, searching for an old man to emerge from the sea of faces. I wanted my father to tell me he'd been watching from afar in the stands, as I stood as salutatorian and gave the senior address.

But as I stepped off the podium with diploma in hand, the crowds dispersed, and no such man came to shake my hand. Our family didn't own a camera, but thank goodness, a youth leader from church came to snap some photos, and that's how I have pictures of me in cap and gown.

That was the day I no longer wished for my father. Later that fall, I climbed onto an airplane to fly to UCLA to start college, and I stopped such childish daydreaming. I was a woman now.

My childhood officially over, Bah-Ba was as good as gone. My Heavenly Father was my only Abba. And that was fine by me.

• • •

As I prepared to meet Kam Lee, I couldn't shake the memory of my father eating his pastry. Or how I once tried to prank him by rubbing his toothbrush across a bar of soap, telling him I helped prepare his toothbrush with toothpaste. I'll never forget the explosion of coughing and howling that erupted, sending his glasses flying off the bridge of his nose as he expelled the ghastly glob of suds from his mouth in a panic. He emerged from the bathroom with boyish admiration and congratulated me. "You got Daddy!"

Wouldn't it be great to simply eject from your head the thought of someone who broke your heart? What good is it to remember that ex-boyfriend who was bad for you, the girlfriend who stabbed your back, or the family member who was just too broken to stop hurting you?

But underneath all the vows to bury what was dead, a truth still beat alive, like a flame lighting the corner of the room. *You miss them.* You're wounded because you never grieved the loss they left inside you.

I couldn't admit this to myself, but my body was telling a different story. Every two hours at night, I was jolted awake, gripped by choking panic attacks, heart palpitations pounding like a jackhammer. My throat narrowed and chest tightened, so I couldn't breathe.

I lay awake, blinking with insomnia, so exhausted that even my eye sockets hurt. My therapist said it wasn't the adult me experiencing these symptoms, but the little girl in me who always hid behind the steel trapdoor of her heart, but was now surfacing, safe to feel it all now. God was bringing me back into my past because my faith was now strong enough to bear the healing that would come from confessing my grief:

I miss you, Daddy.
Don't you love me?
Why did you leave me?

I needed to know why my daddy left.

I am a practical girl. I didn't go to find my father because I wanted him back in my life. I went because I needed to fill in the blanks of my past, to live fully in the present. My journey of homecoming couldn't be complete unless I returned to love. Even if my heart broke again, I knew I must return. For without love, I was not whole.

We cannot truly belong anywhere if we cannot be at home with our grief for those we've loved and those we've lost. Grief opens doorways in our hearts to rooms we once sectioned off with yellow caution tape because we were afraid of our anger, confusion, and sadness. We step into the barricaded areas we've cordoned off to discover that underneath all that sorrow is something beautiful, like the cleansing warmth of sunlight: love.

We must walk each other home, friend. No matter what answers we discover. Because when we finally find the courage to face our grief, we honor a beautiful part of living: loving and being loved. We live fully human. We become more like Jesus, who fully loved each person who deserted Him. We will finally be present in the moment.

We will be able to speak in our own voice, even as it breaks. That moment will be ours. And that moment will be home.

> You are precious to me, and I have given you a special place
> of honor. I love you (Isaiah 43:4 ERV).

LETTER TO MY YOUNGER SELF
You Are Worthy of Honoring Your Grief

Beloved,

You have permission to love and miss the people you miss.

Honor your journey. Honor the truth. You have permission to cherish a memory, to grieve a memory, even if it broke your heart. Because there in the soil of your grief, your heart will come alive and want to love and be loved again.

Your grieving is like releasing your breath—it's the inhale and exhale of your soul. We have to grieve what we've lost, and then we can be free to be who God has called us to be.

Return to love, for there God's heart is beating with yours, holding you close, honoring your pain.

ART OF CHINESE SEAL CARVING

The Chinese art of seal carving (or chop art) is one of the traditional four arts, including painting, calligraphy, and poetry. A typical seal is carved on a small block of stone using a special knife to inscribe a person's name in calligraphy, conveying ownership of a document, piece of art, or literary work. First introduced as early as 1600 BC during the Shang Dynasty, it was used by the emperor to authenticate his word.

Since ancient times, artists have signed their paintings using their chop in red ink, like a stamp. Some paintings from ancient China have over 20 seal marks. The marks do not take away value from the painting but can actually increase the price, depending on who purchased the painting over the years.[1]

As you honor your losses, you'll not only celebrate how you've loved bravely, but you'll see your loving Savior tenderly carrying you through. God understands the cost of loving someone. So, don't leave your moments of grief locked away in your heart with only broken words of hurt and pain. Open your heart so God's words of love and comfort can imprint His whispers of rest and peace. For you are sealed by the loving presence of God's Holy Spirit even when you are bereft, with no words for your grief (Ephesians 1:13).

Reflect and Share

- *What would you say to your younger self at 18?*

- *What is the grief to which God may be inviting you to open your heart in order to step into the next chapter of your life?*

- *What was something you hoped for when you graduated or looked to adulthood?*

Chapter 25

Scars

In the dead of winter in February, plum blossoms bloom.

As a little girl, I knew spring was coming when huge buckets of plum branches budding with pink petals began filling storefront stands in the produce markets. The plum tree is special to the Chinese people because it blossoms in winter. The plum blossoms signify spring's arrival, symbolizing perseverance and hope.

Spring also meant it was Chinese New Year—one of the most important holidays for Chinese people. The Lunar New Year kicks off the Spring Festival—my favorite time of the year. Tradition calls for loads of sweet candy trays to be set out in the living room in broad daylight, and all the adults to encourage their kids to gobble the candy at will—to invite sweetness to flourish in the new year. But what I loved most was seeing the dreariness of the city streets transformed into a wonderland of blooming flowers.

Holding Ah-Ma's hand, I squeezed with her through the crowded sidewalk of shoppers. It was so endearing to see everyone—no matter how old, young, poor, rich, or carefree—carrying plum blossoms in their arms like a beloved newborn baby. It told me that beauty signified something important to everyone: hope.

Workers stacked plump, shiny, orange tangerines—held together in clusters—into pyramid-like displays. Tangerines symbolized blessings and good fortune.

So, early one Saturday morning in spring, I loaded a cluster of tree-fresh tangerines—with stem and leaves still intact to symbolize good health and fortune—and a pink box of Chinese pastries that included a coconut éclair into the car trunk. These were my welcome gifts for my father. For my Bah-Ba.

I wanted these gifts to be a sign I wished him well, a symbol of respect. As Eric drove through streets I never knew, made up of ranch houses and white picket fences, I counted the house numbers. I told him to stop at an egg-yolk yellow home with clean windows and white trim. The neighborhood we snaked through was so different from the one I grew up walking through—the one littered with broken curbs and beat-up cars propped up on cement blocks.

This was a nice neighborhood. Lawns trimmed. Houses square and tucked in. Not what I expected.

I stepped out of our SUV and onto the sidewalk to greet the father I hadn't seen in 34 years. My father stood in the driveway, waiting for me to arrive. Although his hair was nearly all white, I saw the way he rested his weight slightly on one hip, his head slightly tilted to one side.

I recognize this man. This man was my daddy.

I was no longer the grown-up Bonnie, but little girl Bonnie walking up his pristine driveway. I cried the moment I saw him, standing there with my bag of tangerines and box of baked goods, my tears choking me as my heart was breaking open again. I could not stop sobbing, nor could I speak.

Why did you leave me?!

The words screamed inside my head, but I didn't say a thing. The nice, neat script of questions I had prepared to ask my dad like an investigative journalist disappeared, and I was no longer in control of the torrent of emotions tearing through my mind, body, and soul.

His wife, a slim Chinese woman standing next to him, with her hair pulled back in a bun, broke the silence, saying hello like a restaurant hostess and asking us to come in. She walked us through the open garage door as we took off our shoes and moved through a maze of rooms to the living room, where my father and I sat down across from each other.

"Thank you for letting me come visit," I began. But this only made me cry even harder, because it felt so pitiful to thank him for letting me see him. I was bawling—the kind where you can't control your breathing, and you curl over because your gut feels punched. Your body feels like it has caught on fire, sweat gushing out of your every pore.

I tried to compose myself and used up half the box of Kleenex his wife passed to me, while my helpless husband, who couldn't understand a word of Chinese, sat next to me, soothing my back with his hand. All the while, two apparent strangers—my dad and his wife—stared at me, waiting for me say something.

How could I speak when the only words echoing in my head were, *Where have you been? Didn't you care about me?!*

Instead, I smiled weakly with eyes so puffy that I felt like one of the poor souls Bruce Lee put away with his flying fists as he eliminated them on the temple floor in *Enter the Dragon*. I said through a stuffy nose, "You look the same. Just as I remember you."

He didn't say anything. So I asked him, "Do you recognize me?"

My father slowly raised his eyes to look at me. He began to slowly shake his head.

"No," he answered.

My father doesn't recognize me. He doesn't even know me.

I looked up at the door. Could I just get up and leave right then and there? But the door was secured by a series of locks that I wouldn't know how to get through quickly enough for a clean exit. Plus, my shoes were still sitting on the other side of the house, and surely, Eric and I could not leave in our socks.

What happened next can best be described as a catastrophic natural event, like the Mount St. Helen's eruption—an explosion of questions discharging from the deep core of my soul.

"Why did you leave? Why didn't you write? Did you ever think about me or even miss me? I looked for you when I graduated from high school, but you never came." My chest was hurting so bad from pushing down my sobs that I could hardly get the words out coherently. My speech sputtered like a toy car on the last of its batteries.

My father's eyes were cast down, staring at the Kleenex box on the coffee table between us.

"Did you know I grew up poor? I didn't have money to see the doctor. I had to take care of my Ah-Ma and sister. No one to help me."

His response to all these questions was one and the same: "That's the way your mother wanted it."

I noticed all around us, displayed on the walls and in picture frames decorating the shelves on the TV console, stood pictures of his new family—his son and his wife. Family vacations, high school and college graduation.

This guy's built a whole other life without me just fine. Preserve whatever dignity you have left. Begin your exit strategy, I told myself.

I went into my polite guest mode and addressed him in English. "You have nice pictures of your family and your son. Does he live nearby?"

"Yes!" my father nodded enthusiastically, suddenly coming to life. He told me all about his son, what he majored in at college, that he married recently, that he bought his home, that he had a good job. Yet not once during this entire conversation did my father ask anything about me or my family.

"Well, I should be going." I thanked him and his wife for their time.

"Okay. Take care. Bye," my father said at the doorway.

As we drove away, I sat in the passenger seat, empty-handed. My father had prepared no gifts for me. And I swore I never wanted to see him again.

* * *

When I was little, no more than two years old, Ah-Ma told me I had stepped out of our house and decided to run as fast as I could away from her, barreling down the slanted streets of San Francisco outside our doorstep. Since my little legs could not keep up with the acceleration of gravity as I flew down the street, I tripped, falling head-long at breakneck speed onto the concrete sidewalk, helpless to break my fall.

I broke my chin open, and blood gushed everywhere. According to Ah-Ma, the first thing she did was check to see if my front teeth had busted loose and how badly I had bit my tongue. Even though you could literally see the doors of the Chinese Hospital across the street on the next block, we couldn't afford to go there.

So, Ah-Ma scooped me up, doubled back her steps to go home, and ran up a flight of stairs to ask her mother-in-law what to do. Ah-Ma claimed my grandma Mah-Mah stuck her hand in a package of C&H sugar and placed a clump of sugar in the gaping hole right between my lower lip and my chin to stem the bleeding. Mah-Mah said that's how they did it back in the old country. Pouring sugar into a bloody, open wound would help it clot and fight infection. So, instead of getting stitches or today's surgical glue to sew me back up, I had a granulated sugar poultice packed into my chin, and everyone called it good.

The result of this emergency home medical intervention is that I inherited a scar that sits like a long hyphen on my chin. Friends at school and well-meaning coworkers in meetings would gesture and not so subtly send me hand signals to brush food off my chin. I'd tell them about my accidental turn as a tumbling acrobat on the streets of Chinatown and thank them kindly.

We all carry scars, and the deepest ones are always the ones that are invisible, that have formed over the pain in our hearts. Each scar tells a story.

● ● ●

I don't want this scar. I drove out to hike a trail early the next morning, and high in a spot in the mountains, I sobbed against an old oak tree.

I thought this was Your will, God, leading me to find my father. But what was the point of breaking my heart a second time? This was cruel, I told God. *Why?*

As God gently comforted me, like a loving father comforts a child when she stumbles and falls. God was holding me in His presence as I cried in pain. God couldn't tell me that very moment why He allowed my story to carry such a scar.

Just like a child doesn't cry after first skinning her knee, refusing the help of nearby strangers, but ends up wailing like kingdom come once her daddy or mommy runs over to scoop her up, I was the little girl overwhelmed with her sadness. All my anger, loneliness, and confusion poured out to my Heavenly Father. I found safety wrapped in His loving arms as He embraced me.

Now, I really don't belong to anyone. I don't have any history. I had already lost the mother I wished to have. Now, I had no father either.

I'm an orphan. Belonging to no one.

I looked up into the sky, my vision blurring with tears. Then, I remembered how Jesus was resurrected with scars still visible. Jesus did not hide His body or His heart from the pain, brutality, and violence. He willingly yielded Himself to the unimaginable, so that we don't have to face the unimaginable alone.

Jesus embraced His past instead of erasing it. His scars held tremendous beauty and value. It was Jesus's scars that the disciple Thomas needed to touch in order to truly believe Jesus was someone real.

Our scars are made beautiful as Jesus folds His hands into ours and whispers, "I have redeemed you; I have summoned you by name; you are mine" (Isaiah 43:1). He put me on His strong shoulders and carried me as I collapsed from the weight of my nothingness. *What do I have to give to my children? What legacy will I give them? Will I have no stories but broken ones to pass on, like what was passed on to me?*

As God's heart broke in a thousand pieces with mine, I heard Him whisper, "You are My daughter. This story we have lived through together shall be our song. You are My story, and My story is in you."

God is the only one who shares my every memory and witnessed every experience and heartache.

I see You now, Jesus.

I thought I was all alone, belonging to no one.

But I see clearly now. It has always been You.

You have always been with me.
Quietly, faithfully, You have been loving me.

I cried bittersweet tears of joy because I realized that one day, when my children read my broken story, they will understand what it means when I tell them, "God is your home." When you open the doors you were never allowed to open, when you can no longer deny your truth, when you finally walk into the reality of your one beautiful life, you will find Jesus tenderly holding you, folding His hand into yours.

I didn't know it at the time, but my scars would lead me to something more beautiful than I ever imagined. My scars would no longer be a flaw I needed to hide, but would be transformed into a gift to embrace.

I would soon learn that the missing pieces were the spaces needed to complete the mosaic of God's great love for me.

> "Behold, I make all things new...Write, for these words are true and faithful" (Revelation 21:5 NKJV).

 ## LETTER TO MY YOUNGER SELF
You Are Worthy of Renewal

Beloved,

There is nothing God cannot rebuild, remake, and renew with beauty.

The truth of your scars and your story is your home. For there, in your humanity, your Savior is gathering you in His loving arms to make you new again.

Jesus whispers, "I am My beloved's. And My beloved is Mine."

TANGERINES

Tangerines are a gift that symbolize a blessing to friends and loved ones during the Chinese New Year. The more stems and green leaves there are, the more these tangerines invite vibes of fertility and prosperity to go your way, to make your new year fruitful. In Chinese, the word *tangerines* is pronounced "gum gut," which is a homonym for *gold* and *luck*. Chinese people believe in the power of words, and they display tangerines in their homes for 14 days to celebrate the Lunar New Year, ushering in newness and good fortune through the doorway to settle on the family. As daughters of our loving God, His words breathe new life, making all things new in our souls with the fruitfulness of peace, joy, faith, hope, and love. But the greatest of these is love, and because we have God's love, we are a blessing wherever we go.

Reflect and Share

- *What would you tell your younger self about her scars?*

- *How is God making you new?*

- *What story do your scars tell?*

Chapter 26

Dim Sum

I pointed to a shop in front of us—shuttered, boarded up, its awning stripped of logo and name, like faded summer tan lines aging in winter. *Tung Fong.*

"That's where Ah-Ma took me to have dim sum every day," I told Eric.

This was one of the happiest places on earth for me as a child. *Tung Fong* means "The Eastern Way," and it was the name of a Hong Kong teahouse. I loved stepping into the bright, sunlit room as a little girl. It was filled with the savory smells of steamed pork spareribs in black bean sauce and barbecue pork buns, called *cha-siu bau*. This was my favorite part of the day, when Ah-Ma and I stopped to rest and refresh and have dim sum.

Dim sum translates as "touch of heart," and refers to delicious, bite-sized, tapas-like dishes freshly made just a few feet away from you in the kitchen, where half a dozen hands artfully make each one that you place in your mouth. Dim sum is shared among family and friends at the table, people pausing for a cup of tea, with plates of hors d'oeuvres spread in front of them. Chopsticks clink on a small plate as you swirl soy sauce into a dash of garlic chili paste, like a painter's palette for your delicacies.

Dim sum is served on little plates placed in carts that servers push by your table. You call out the names of the dish to get it delivered to you, like *har gow*, which means you'll be crunching bits of shrimp wrapped in translucent tapioca-wheat flour dumplings. A dim sum *sifu* master chef expertly flutes the dough into beautiful edges, like a baker finishing a piecrust, to seal in the juices with artistic, quick precision as the dish cooks piping hot in bamboo steamers.

Instead of windows nailed over with plywood, I saw the big, beautiful, gleaming round windows I had peered into as a little girl, watching slender, mascara-lipstick-wearing young ladies push steaming food carts, serving dishes, and replenishing teapots for smartly dressed customers. These waitresses dressed in crisp, white aprons wore matching ruffled headbands like tiaras in their hair, looking cute and smart in their uniforms, complete with white sneakers, like servers from a '60s diner.

The great thing about dim sum is you can order a little or a lot. Dim sum can be a meal or a simple treat, depending on your mood and how much time you have. I loved having dim sum as a little girl because Ah-Ma was always happy there, and the waitresses doted on me as surrogate aunties.

For a few moments, I was their favorite niece, asking me to sing them songs, which I happily obliged. They often slipped me a Chinese dessert on the house, like my favorite: classic Hong Kong Black Sesame Rolls (芝麻卷), which are like jelly roll cakes, except instead of flour, the layers are made of Jell-O-like sheets of fragrant, ground black sesame mixed with water chestnut flour and sweetened with rock sugar. My other favorite, even to this day, is crispy sesame balls, which are deep-fried, glutinous rice balls, filled with sweet lotus seed paste and rolled in toasted white sesame.

But what I really love about dim sum is the tea. You just can't gulp hot tea. You have to sip and savor. It comes out boiling hot, so fragrant, with so many different varieties to request. Before you even pull out a chair to sit down, the waitress asks, "What tea will you drink?"

Ah-Ma always ordered Pu-Er tea, which she explained was the healthiest tea, rich in antioxidants, known to cut cholesterol and clean the body of toxins. But, sometimes, the waitresses asked Ah-Ma, "How about trying jasmine today? It's a beautiful tea."

The word *beautiful* jumped out at me. In Chinese, the word for jasmine tea means "fragrant leaf." So enticing. "Can we try jasmine?" I asked my mother.

I didn't get to taste jasmine tea as a little girl with my dim sum at the teahouse. And I didn't expect to find it in a mostly unlikely place: when we visited an elderly friend in Chinatown.

· · ·

Cheung Po-Po, or Grandma Cheung as friends affectionately called her, lived in one of the eight-by-ten-foot single room occupancy (SRO) tenements in Chinatown, where residents have to walk down a hallway to use a communal bathroom and kitchen. Every now and then, Ah-Ma and I visited Cheung Po-Po. She was a widow and distant relative of a distant relative, and for immigrants, any person with any kind of connection back home was coveted company.

Grandma Cheung was really old. She had moles all over her face, and you could tell she lived a hard life, as told by the innumerable lines crisscrossing her visage. She always wore a polyester pant and shirt set, with layers of sweater vests she knit herself, though her nails were thick, and the skin on her fingers cracked from lack of care. Although it seemed she was someone a little girl might be wary of, I enjoyed visiting Grandma Cheung very much because she had sparkly, dancing eyes that smiled and a voice that sang like a brook whenever she laughed, which was about every other sentence.

Not only was Grandma Cheung jovial, but she always showed an interest in me, asking questions about all kinds of things she remembered from our previous conversations. I noticed that on her dresser, next to her tofu-sized folding TV tray, she placed an arrangement of various black-and-white framed pictures of her children and grandchildren. Her husband had died when she was very young. Grandma Cheung looked flawless in youth, glowing inside and out.

Whenever we visited, she would pad over to her large steel thermos of hot water, retrieve three Chinese porcelain floral painted teacups from the dish drying rack, open a tin can of dried tea, and make tea for us.

Though we sat there huddled in her small room, the fragrance of her hot tea, warm in my hands, filled the room, as she shared stories and folksy encouragement. Her tea felt smooth in my mouth, and I loved the scent as I brought the cup close to my lips. Holding her teacup made me feel pretty, just like the handful of spring flowers she crocheted. She placed her handcrafted petals along the top of her dresser, decorating the picture frames of her family.

She saw me admiring them. She brought them down to let me see. "Do you like these? Here, pick one." I didn't know if Ah-Ma would let me, but Grandma Cheung picked a pink flower and placed it in my hand. "The pink one is for you. It is beautiful. Like you."

The delicate, intricately handmade pink flower was one of the most beautiful gifts I have ever received.

I thanked her and added that I loved the tea.

"You like it? It's jasmine tea."

"Yes, I like jasmine tea." I replied. "It's sweet."

When we got home, Ah-Ma told me to throw the flower away. It was old, worn, and dirty—why would I want something so raggedy around? "She just gave it to you because you kept looking at it. If you keep old, ugly things around, you'll get used to living with old, ugly things."

I don't have that little pink flower anymore. But after all these years, I still remember with fondness how that crocheted flower felt in my hand. I wish I had kept it.

Sorrow might seem like it's not very useful in our lives. We just want to get rid of it, like ugly, old things in our lives getting dusty on top of a dresser. But like petals of spring flowers, those moments of sorrow tell us that something beautiful and significant once existed in our heart. When we try to erase our sorrow, like it never happened, we also lose sight of those beautiful moments of clarity that are meaningful to us.

Even though you, and only you, know the meaning they hold, those glimmers of joy and hope connected to those hard parts of your life are treasures, like the little picture frames of memories Grandma Cheung cherished next to her dusty crocheted flowers.

> I have trusted in Your loving devotion; my heart will rejoice in Your salvation. I will sing to the Lord, for He has been good to me (Psalm 13:6 BSB).

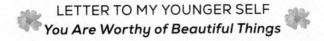

LETTER TO MY YOUNGER SELF
You Are Worthy of Beautiful Things

Beloved,

Sadness and sorrow will give you a special gift to recognize beauty all around you.

Your challenge will be to believe that those beautiful things—the stars set in the night sky, the little blade of grass your children will pick to give you—were inspired by the touch of God's hand for you to receive.

When you dare to believe that God was thinking of your smile as He brings you the spring rain, and as you notice its first droplets tapping on your windowpane, the world will be a little brighter. You'll find you have a place in this world among the beautiful things.

DIM SUM

Dim sum is considered the quintessential Cantonese cuisine—a thousand-year-old tradition of travelers stopping to rest and refresh along the Silk Road and to enjoy delicately made food while drinking tea—a celebrated custom called *yum chai*. Teahouses sprang up along trade routes in the southern China Guangzhou region—a bustling port where international visitors passed through.

Dim sum is special because the focus isn't on eating to satisfy hunger, but to enjoy the beautiful attention to detail used to prepare each small dish. Each dim sum dish is meant to be enjoyed slowly and admired for the skill that the dim sum *sifu* master chef expended in handcrafting each delicacy. The goal of dim sum is to leisurely spend time enjoying conversation and each other's company, pouring tea for each other, strengthening the bonds of friendship and family.

In the same way, life becomes beautiful again when we stop along the road of life to rest and refresh by sharing conversation among friends and family. We remember that when we take time to share the tiny details of life, our souls become reenergized. We see beautiful things growing in the soil of our daily lives. Life can be sweet again.

Reflect and Share

- *What would you tell your younger self about the importance of beauty in her life?*

- *How is God inspiring you to add more beauty into your life?*

- *What was your happy place as a child that made the world a beautiful place for you? Was there an experience in your life that made you doubt the importance of beauty for you?*

Chapter 27

The Cup

I was seven years old, attending my first church evangelistic retreat at a conference center in the mountains. My parents had just finalized their divorce, and Ah-Ma was feeling isolated as a single parent. Because Chinese people back then often felt drawn to the church as a place to find a community of people who spoke their language, Ah-Ma began attending church.

A pastor had called our home. Somehow, he had heard through the grapevine that my grandparents, aunts, and uncles had newly immigrated, and we were all living together.

Something in the way this pastor spoke to Ah-Ma on the phone intrigued her, and I soon found myself wandering the grounds around the building where the gospel evangelistic meeting was taking place. Back in the '70s, there was no children's program. All the kids sat in the back of the church, waiting for the service to be over so we could descend in a horde around the snack table, run around, and play tag.

All the sermons given in Chinese about the Bible sounded boring to me. Because Scripture translated in Chinese is very formal, I didn't understand what was being said. But that night, there was a guest speaker. He was young, and he didn't talk in *Thees* and *Thous*. He spoke in regular, plain, everyday, conversational Chinese.

Something else was different about this preacher. He was telling a *story*. I was thoroughly captivated.

The preacher said that once upon a time, there was a prince of a big, beautiful kingdom. Because he was the prince, the people in his kingdom did not really know him. The people served him, but they did not feel comfortable being too close to the prince.

But the prince loved the people and decided that the only way he could be close to them was to become one of them.

The prince left the palace to live among them as a poor, everyday person working the hard life alongside them, so they would grow to know and trust him. The prince loved spending time with them, becoming their best friend, and he helped them all the time with everything.

But one day, the prince was wrongly accused of a crime. Instead of rushing over to stand by the prince, all his friends abandoned him. No one spoke up to defend him. The prince was dragged to court and condemned to die as a criminal.

As an avid reader, I already guessed what would happen next. The protagonist would stand up, deliver a soliloquy, and reveal his true identity. All would end well, and everyone would live happily ever after.

But this was not how the story went. The protagonist hardly said anything. I was horrified.

The hero of this story dies? What kind of a story is this? I did not like this story at all. It confused me. There was nothing beautiful or meaningful that made any sense. It broke my heart to imagine the loving prince abandoned by everyone he loved, when no one came to his side. Tears started streaming down my face as I imagined him beat up, hungry, tired, thirsty, and bloodied.

Then the preacher told us this was a *true* story. That this Prince who died had a name, and His name was Jesus. His name in Chinese is *Yeshu*. Jesus was the Son of God, and He came down from heaven because becoming a human being was the only way we could know how much He loved us.

That's when something happened inside me that I cannot explain. When I heard that this Jesus was willing to go through the pain of becoming human—of being slapped, whipped, dragged around, ridiculed, spit on, with no one coming to His rescue—something deep and broken inside me cried out.

I started sobbing uncontrollably, as my whole heart felt struck with a thick, aching, dark kind of loneliness that filled my chest, as I imagined Jesus hanging on the cross by Himself, with no one to turn to. Not even His Heavenly Father. Betrayed by His closest friends.

Jesus was all alone. The Jesus I first met was *lonely*.

As the tears streamed down my face, these words poured out of my heart that night, like a frozen river in winter—erupting, running swiftly, melting in spring.

I'm so lonely, Jesus! I'm all alone!

The preacher said that the story did not end there. Because the Prince was both God and man, He did not stay buried and dead. Jesus rose again the third day so He could live in our hearts and love us forever, never to be separated or far away from us anymore. Nothing would ever come between us and God's love ever again. Jesus had gone to heaven to build us each a new home. One day, we would be reunited with Him again.

"All you need to do is open your heart," the preacher said. "Will you believe?"

Yes. I believe. Jesus's suffering loneliness for me meant He loved me. This was pain Jesus understands. If there is a God, and He did this all for me, that was love I could trust.

The preacher asked if anyone believed and wanted to start a new life with Jesus. I stood to walk down the aisle to the front of the church, no longer walking alone, but hand in hand with Jesus.

Jesus, if there is a loving God in this world, it must be You.

I don't want to be alone in this world.

I trust You. I need Your love.

Be Lord of my life.

Come in my heart. I believe.

I prayed this prayer to ask Jesus into my life in Chinese. The story of the gospel that struck into the very core of my being was told to me in Chinese. The soul and spirit God created anew that night, when He first told me He loved me through the power of the Holy Spirt, was birthed in the very identity I tried to throw away.

• • •

One dark night, 2,000 years ago, Jesus rescued me from loneliness to adopt me as His very own, to call me God's beloved daughter. Jesus drank the bitter cup of loneliness Himself that night as He hung on the cross: alone, betrayed, separated from His Heavenly Father. No one comforted Him as He cried out, "Why have You forsaken Me, Father?"

Jesus suffered this unspeakable loneliness so I don't have to suffer in my culture of loneliness anymore.

I thought of my friends Marie and Thomas, who adopted a little girl from China. They're keeping a collection of photos they took of their baby girl at the orphanage when they first met her. Preserving their daughter's adoption story is their invaluable gift to her. Her adoption story testifies that she is a real person, with a real history, born in a specific time and place.

My Heavenly Father was doing the same for me too, by placing my birth certificate on my path again, so I would return to Chinatown.

Reclaiming my past wasn't simply about recapturing my cultural heritage. God was restoring my spiritual heritage—the story of how God adopted me. How I ended up being born in America was part of my God story. I realized God was helping me put together my spiritual adoption story by bringing me back to Chinatown.

Homecoming never felt closer.

> The Spirit you received brought about your adoption...by him we cry, "Abba, Father." The Spirit himself testifies with our spirit that we are God's children (Romans 8:15-16).

LETTER TO MY YOUNGER SELF
You Are Valued

Beloved,

You are wanted. You are desired and valued.

On the darkest night, you found yourself holding a cup of brokenness, filled up with many things in your life that didn't make sense. God made a way to love and adopt you as His beautiful daughter. Jesus drank the cup of loneliness, so you don't have to drink it anymore.

Brokenness isn't the end of your story. God's love is. Everything broken leads you to everything beautiful. Because in everything broken, Jesus has adopted you and given you His name.

Surely goodness and mercy will follow you and your children all the days of your life. God will fill your cup with His love as your Heavenly Father, and His blessings will overflow, running over, because you belong to Him.

THE ART OF ENJOYING CHINESE TEA

The art of Chinese tea goes back 5,000 years when it was first discovered for its ability to awaken and refresh, as well as its medicinal properties. Drinking tea continued to play an important role in Chinese culture as a way of welcoming guests into your home by offering a cup of tea, as a daily practice to nurture your spirit by restoring calm to the body, or even by being enjoyed as an art form. The darker, tangled, unfinished quality of the tea belies the rarity of these older, antique-aged leaves.[1]

Archaeological digs have uncovered Chinese teacups from as far back as the Ming Dynasty, decorated beautifully—handpainted treasures that survived that era.

In the same way, our brokenness, steeped in God's love, becomes a priceless, fragrant offering, served from a beautiful porcelain teacup that holds a delicate rare tea. You are exquisite, like fine china, releasing the personality, body, and rich flavors developed from the stories you've journeyed through over the years.

Reflect and Share

- *What would you tell your younger self about loneliness and what God values about her?*

- *What changes can you make to address feelings of loneliness or to feel more emotionally connected to Jesus?*

- *What is your spiritual adoption story? What drew you to believe in God's love for you and invite Him into your life?*

Chapter 28

Cable Car

Two years after I swore I would never see my earthly father again, I dialed Kam Lee's phone. I wanted to ask Bah-Ba how he ended up here in America. This information was a key part of my adoption story as God's beloved daughter.

This time when I called him, I spoke in a new voice, as the beloved daughter of my Heavenly Abba. I wanted the little girl in me to have her God story, so I could pass my spiritual adoption story to my boys as a legacy to them. This was their spiritual heritage too.

"Bah-Ba? It's Bonnie." I got straight to the point. "I never got to tell you the last time we met, but I am a writer. I want to write about my life, my Chinese American story. But I need to talk to you because I want to learn how you came to America and why you came."

My father's swift reply surprised me. "Ask me anything."

"I'm sorry I haven't called after we last met. I was hurt you didn't come back for me. I needed time to think through everything. I want you to know I forgive you. I am not angry at you."

The phone line went quiet, so I kept going. "I became a Christian when I was a little girl. And even though it was really hard growing up, Jesus—who is God—helped me. He made me strong. I graduated from college and went on to study engineering and work in high tech. Then, God led me to meet a loving man, and I'm married now with two boys. So I am very blessed."

"That's good," my father interjected.

"I just have a lot of missing holes in my story, which always made me sad." I felt braver, speaking more boldly in this new interchange. "I want my boys to have a full story of their lives. And I'm even writing a book about my Asian American journey."

"Hmm," my father parlayed.

Then, I did something I did not plan to do until that very second.

"Would you like to come over to my house for lunch?" I asked. "I want you to meet Josh and Caleb, so they can know their Yeh-Yeh." I wanted to break the legacy of secrets and shame passed down to me. I wanted my children to meet their biological grandpa. I wanted to sing a new song of freedom as the daughter of my beloved Heavenly Father, and somehow this lunch formed its first lyrics. "Then, if you don't mind, can I ask you questions about how you came to the U.S., when your family came, how you met my mom, got married, and then divorced?"

My father liked this invitation. "Yes, of course. Anything you want to ask me, I'll tell you. Yes, I'd like to come see your kids."

Can you imagine how shocked my boys were when I sat them down and told them that, for the first time ever, they would be meeting my father?

"What? Your *father* is coming?! He's still alive? When did you find him?" A million questions ensued. I always told my kids my father left me when I seven, and I never saw him again. I never told Josh and Caleb about my first reunion with my father because I wanted to shield them from the pain of rejection. But here I was, telling them the whole story now. To my shock, my kids, instead of being sad for me, were amazed by what I was doing.

"Wow, Mom! You're so brave!" I did not anticipate this response. When I explained that this was just a one-time meeting, to simply learn about my history, that I was not committing to an ongoing relationship with my father, Josh and Caleb got it.

"Of course, Mom. We understand." Who are these kids? Are these the same boys who fight over what to watch during screen time? "You should ask your dad *all* your questions! We support you!"

Here I was worried that they would be emotionally confused.

We work so hard to shield our children from our pain, but what they really need is to understand our pain. When we nurture our children with our love and feed their souls with our stories, our children become wise sojourners, kindred spirits on the journey of life with us. They begin to capture the wonder of God's mysterious work in the stories of our lives, instead of observing faith in a sterile, clean room of spiritual clichés.

By seeing clearly the vibrant complexities of the human experience and the details of how we fall down in our weaknesses and get back up with God's healing love for our strength, they see how God becomes flesh in you and me. *We gain their trust.* We become someone they can confide in honestly about their journey of faith as a human too.

"Remember to be polite, loving, caring, and kind," I admonished the boys. "Mom has forgiven this person. God has used what was meant for bad for good."

"Yes! Just like God did for Joseph," they chimed back. It was a refrain I've always guided them by, whenever they faced tough times. Now, they were singing back in chorus with me too.

I gathered them close for a big hug, and I asked them, "Will you pray for me?" Together, we encircled each other, linking arms in a group prayer. The ground we stood on transformed into holy ground.

We started tidying the house before I drove out to pick my father up and bring him to our home. God was about to reorient the story of my life.

. . .

I never knew there was a whole other world outside the half-mile perimeter of San Francisco Chinatown. As Ah-Ma walked the length of this small world, her hand became my whole world. I went wherever she took me. I never ventured away.

I never saw the city lights along Nob Hill. Why? Because Ah-Ma and I never walked past California Street, which marked the western boundary of Chinatown. Anything beyond this line did not exist for me.

But that morning as I drove to pick up my father, I was letting go of Ah-Ma's hand, to go and find the answers I had been seeking my whole life.

● ● ●

With my father sitting less than a few feet from me at the dining table, I diced up some chicken sausage, beat six eggs, poured some vegetable oil in a pan along with steamed rice, and threw in mixed vegetables. I was cooking Chinese Fried Rice for my father.

I stir-fried the ingredients over a sizzling hot pan while Bah-Ba sat close, talking to Josh and Caleb. My kids were chatting with him, and for the first time, I heard my father laugh, asking his grandkids questions any grandpa would. My father was speaking to them in broken, limited English, but it was enough.

"What sports did you play when you were a boy?" big brother Josh asked my father. As I transferred my fried rice from the pan onto a serving platter, counting sets of chopsticks and gathering rice bowls to take to the table, I overheard my father tell my boys he loved playing soccer when he was a young.

Tomboy that I was, I had loved playing soccer at recess with the boys in elementary school. *Interesting.*

My father didn't say much to me at lunch. He was shy, looking down as he ate. He was a chatterbox talking to my kids. Why was he so quiet with me? Why wasn't my father asking me any questions?

After clearing the dishes, I took out my notebook, pen, and iPhone. I asked him if it was okay if I recorded our conversation.

"No problem," he answered. I found his willingness interestingly odd. The man who sat across from me no longer appeared to be my father, but more like a historical character whom I finally got to interview.

"Let me make us some tea." I got up to put a kettle on the stove. I opened the tea drawer and reached to the back, past the chamomile, lavender, and peppermint tea. I took out the Good Earth tea and rooibos so I could reach the tea I had not served in many, many years.

Jasmine tea. I poured tea for my father and me.

"Thank you." He brought the cup to his lips, his shoulders relaxed, and an exhale opened the space between us.

We spent more than three hours talking that afternoon.

• • •

I learned that my dad's grandfather—my great-grandfather—was sold as a slave when he was a little boy and was shipped from China to be a laborer in Hilo, Hawaii.

(I'm going to call my father "Dad" to avoid confusion in the storytelling that follows.)

My dad's grandfather died in 1951 and was buried in Hawaii. My dad brought out an envelope from his coat pocket and set it on the table. He pulled out pictures of my great-grandfather's grave that my dad had visited to pay his respects by burning incense and paper money.

"Was your father born in Hawaii, then?" I was incredulous. How did my dad end up in Hong Kong instead of Hawaii?

"No. My father, named Le Ning, was born in China after my grandfather returned to China to marry a woman from his village. There were no Chinese women to marry in America. Chinese people were prohibited from immigrating then. So, my grandfather had to go back to China to get a wife. He had a son, who is my father."

So my grandfather Yeh-Yeh was born in China. I asked why my great-grandfather didn't bring his wife and his son (my grandfather Yeh-Yeh) to live with him in Hawaii.

"Too poor. No money to bring them both to Hawaii. He just worked and sent money home to my father," my dad replied.

Then, my dad dropped a bombshell on me.

"Your great-grandfather—my grandfather—became a U.S. citizen in Hawaii. He became a postmaster and became very wealthy," my father explained. It turns out that my great-grandfather became a naturalized U.S. citizen when Hawaii became a U.S. territory in 1908 to establish Pearl Harbor as a naval base.

Wait a minute. *My great-grandfather was a U.S. citizen? What?*

"Why weren't you rich then?" I was dumbfounded. This was getting more intriguing by the minute.

My dad explained. "My grandfather eventually raised enough money to send for my father, Le Ning, to reunite with him in Hawaii. My father was 40 years old by the time he arrived in Hawaii, only to discover my grandfather had taken a second wife and was raising another set of children. He was living in a big house, raising a whole other family in Hawaii during all those years my father was suffering in poverty back in China." My father recounted plot lines to my grandfather Yeh-Yeh's life that sounded like a soap opera.

"Ai yah!" I exclaimed. "That's awful! What did Yeh-Yeh do?"

"When my father discovered this truth, he felt betrayed and abandoned," my dad said. "They fought and fought. Then, grandfather disinherited him. Cut my father out of his will. A year later, grandfather died in 1951."

My grandfather Yeh-Yeh had been abandoned by his father, who was raising another family in wealth, while Yeh-Yeh grew up in poverty, stripped of his inheritance—and here I was growing up in poverty, abandoned by *my* dad, who was living well, apparently raising another family. The irony was not lost on me.

"Wait a minute. Where were *you* born?" I lost my breath, hardly getting the words out quick enough. "If Yeh-Yeh was an American citizen, does that mean that as his son you've always been an American too?"

"Even though my father was a U.S. citizen, he had to return to his Chinese village to marry and have kids because America still prohibited Chinese immigration. That's why I was born in China instead of America," my dad explained. "I couldn't immigrate to America until 1965, when all quotas against Chinese immigrants ended. That's when my siblings and I reunited with Yeh-Yeh as naturalized citizens, as children of an American citizen. That's when I came to the U.S."

This was mind-shattering, identity-altering truth. It turns out I was not the child of first generation Chinese American immigrants. I am a fourth generation Chinese American!

I learned that my grandfather Yeh-Yeh took a voyage on a ship to San Francisco Chinatown, entering at Angel Island the same year the rest of his family—my dad, his mom, and his siblings—fled to Hong Kong to get away from the Communists taking over China.

"Where did you live in Hong Kong?" I asked.

"Sham Shui Po," my father replied. Sound familiar? It's the *same city* I served during my time as a missionary in Hong Kong. It's amazing. I was walking my father's childhood streets in Hong Kong, serving the at-risk boys there, in the same neighborhoods where he walked as a boy and teenager!

"How did you end up here in San Francisco?" This was the question I'd been waiting to ask all my life.

"John F. Kennedy. The Civil Rights Movement," my dad said. "His law to let all immigrants in was signed in 1965. Before that, Chinese people weren't allowed into the country. But Kennedy supported the Civil Rights Movement. He wanted everyone to come to America."

Wow. I didn't even know my dad was so civic minded. It's true—prior to 1965, Congress restricted naturalized citizenship to those of European descent. For the Chinese, we were the first ethnic group in America to be denied immigration because of the Chinese Exclusionary Act passed into law in 1882, and in effect until 1943. It was repealed when China became a U.S. ally during World War II. However, the discriminatory law was replaced by a quota: Only 105 Chinese immigrants could enter the U.S. per year. All quotas were abolished after President Lyndon Johnson passed immigration reform in 1965 as a tribute to legislation initiated by President John F. Kennedy before his assassination at the height of the Civil Rights Movement. My national identity was intricately woven with the identity of generations of American immigrants.

With immigration restrictions lifted, an influx of Chinese immigrants arrived in the '70s, along with an explosion of Chinese restaurants cropping up coast-to-coast, and that's when my father came by ship and arrived in Chinatown. To become a busboy.

Like his father, and his father before him, my dad returned to Hong Kong to find a wife to marry. That's how he met Ah-Ma. And that's how I ended being born in Chinese Hospital in San Francisco Chinatown.

I started laughing at this new discovery of my national heritage. I'm actually descended from a Chinese American who lived in Hawaii in the late nineteenth century! My father, Kam Lee, was born in 1942—the year after Pearl Harbor was bombed.

My father smiled at me for the first time. "Yes. Our family has been American citizens for a long time."

And I smiled back.

"Your uncle, my big brother, even volunteered to fight in the Vietnam War!" my dad announced with pride. My dad wanted to serve, but he didn't make the weight minimum. But he was proud that his big brother did. "Your uncle Dai-Baak served in the Army on the front lines as combat engineer, clearing booby traps, building bridges so vehicles and troops could get across, building trenches, clearing the path of whatever obstacles the enemy threw at them."

My dad told me that my uncle was very brave and loved being a soldier. Just imagine—my uncle Dai-Baak could have been serving alongside Eric's dad in Vietnam. Maybe my uncle built a bridge that Butch's platoon marched across!

I can't tell you how many cups of tea I poured for us. But I needed to ask my father how the marriage fell apart.

• • •

This is where the story got dicey. I learned there is another version of what happened between my Ah-Ma and my father. Who said what. Who asked whom to leave.

My father told me he didn't want the divorce. Ah-Ma told me he did. My father told me he dated my mom for months before they got married. Ah-Ma said they never dated at all.

And there is more that is not meant to be recorded in these pages.

I wrote it all down on my notepad. I don't know who to believe.

But this I know: A little girl and her baby sister were lost in the scuffle between a husband and wife who became enemies, living difficult, broken, and complex lives. Each of them has flaws. Each of them has hopes and dreams.

• • •

It was getting late, but before we ended our time together, I had one last question: "I'm curious, do you have faith? Do you believe in God?" And there, late one afternoon with my earthly father, I shared the gospel with him.

My dad listened and politely replied, "I'm glad you found your Jesus."

I got up to say, "Thank you so much for spending time and talking about painful things in your life. I really appreciate it. You've helped me know my story, and now I feel at peace."

"Wait. I brought something for you." My dad pulled out a small pocket photo album. "Here are a few pictures of you and me," he said, flipping through just five photos. "These are the only pictures I have of you, because your mom wouldn't let me take any. I gave these photos to your grandmother Mah-Mah. I found them in her drawer after she died."

Five precious pictures taken of us together. In one photo, I am standing next to my father striking a kung fu pose, our fists raised up like Bruce Lee. We were standing on the grass lawn at the Conservatory of Flowers in Golden Gate Park, San Francisco—dad and daughter doing our kung fu.

"You can keep these," my dad said.

Flipping through the album, I found two photos of Ah-Ma and my dad at their Chinese wedding banquet. I had never seen a photo of my mother and father together. Ah-Ma was wearing a red wedding cheongsam silk dress, and she was only 17. I would be born later that year.

"Can I keep these too?" I asked, with tears welling in my eyes.

"Go ahead," my dad replied. "I don't have any use for them. They're yours."

• • •

I drove my father back home.

"Take care of yourself," my father turned to say to me, stepping out of the car.

"You too, Bah-Ba. Take care of yourself." I smiled. I watched him punch in the code to open his garage door, waving one last time before he disappeared.

This time, our goodbye felt different than before. I was truly saying goodbye, like watching the sunset descending on winter's last evening. Waiting for me on the other side of the darkest night sky was the brightest sunrise, walking hand in hand with my real Daddy, my loving Heavenly Abba Father. This time, our goodbye was my heart's homecoming.

Jesus was folding His hand into the hand of the little girl in me. Together, we were walking her home, leaving the broken places, yet carrying all that was beautiful and meaningful with us, to live out in the prairie of open spaces.

As I drove home, watching the evening melt into a halcyon shimmer of crimson, yellow, and orange among feathers of a gray-blue sky, like plumage on the wings of a great blue heron taking flight, I whispered. I whispered just as I had one dark night many years ago as a little girl, hearing the story of a Prince who died and rose again so He could speak my name and adopt me as His.

I whispered, *I believe, Jesus. All I am is Yours. You are home to me.*
I belonged.

> The wilderness and the dry land will be glad; the desert will rejoice and blossom like a rose. It will blossom abundantly (Isaiah 35:1-2 HCSB).

LETTER TO MY YOUNGER SELF
You Are Worthy of Blossoming

Beloved,

Don't give up on her. On that little girl in you. Encourage her to believe there is a place for her to blossom in this world.

Take your time. There is no rush or expiration date to being you. There is room for you to grow and learn what happy looks like in your own way.

Help her take just one next step to bloom right where she is planted. Help her to celebrate and embrace her true worth, because the treasure that Jesus calls the pearl of great price is the real you.

JASMINE TEA

My favorite tea releases a sweet, floral fragrance. Jasmine tea.

Jasmine tea is the most famous scented tea in China. Jasmine is a beautiful white flower that represents purity, beauty, kindness, and eternal love.

Jasmine flowers (茉莉花 *mo li hua*) were appreciated for their fragrance and used in the eighteenth century to decorate and perfume the emperor's rooms. The flowers were also used to imbue a beautiful scent to clothes, and royal women would wear jasmine flowers in their hair.

The jasmine buds in jasmine tea are gathered and placed in the tea leaves. As the buds begin to open, they release their fragrance.

When you pass by jasmine flowers, do you recognize their sweet fragrance? You are like jasmine flowers as daughters of the King. You are beautiful as you open your heart and life to share your stories, releasing the sweet fragrance of Christ wherever you go. Your life—living loved by Jesus—is no longer lonely. Your life is sweet. Sweet like jasmine.

Reflect and Share

- *What would you tell your younger self about God's love for her?*

- *What changes can you make to embrace your true worth as God's beloved daughter?*

- *What is your spiritual adoption story? What drew you to believe in God's love for you and invite Him into your life?*

Chapter 29

Homecoming

As Eric and I crossed the street at the corner of Jackson and Powell, where the uphill climb suddenly tilted steeper, I heard a familiar sound rumbling below ground.

Jackson and Powell is where two out of only three cable car lines—the world's last and only manually operating cable car systems—intersect in San Francisco. Both the Powell-Mason and Powell-Hyde cable cars share the same set of tracks running down Powell Street, beginning their runs at the most-photographed cable car turntable at Market Street near Union Square, where tourists get in line to hop on. Both cable car lines pull passengers uphill past Nob Hill. Once the cable car approaches California Street to enter into Chinatown territory, it gets exciting.

Right there at Jackson Street and Powell, where my childhood home sits, the two cable car lines traveling to different destinations both turn a hard left to go uphill past my home. There, within a small one-block stretch of cable car tracks on Jackson Street, literally right in front of my childhood home (I kid you not), two cable car lines diverge. The Powell-Mason cable car heading to Fisherman's Wharf lurches right onto Mason Street, while the other Powell-Hyde cable hunkers down, ascending up into the sky toward Ghiradelli Square.

Since opening over a hundred years ago in 1888, the Powell-Mason cable car that rumbled past my door has run the exact same route, using the same type of equipment. It's been in operation longer than any other transit line in the world.

Ah-Ma would open the door to start our daily trek down to buy fresh fish and produce and *bam*! Fifteen thousand pounds of steel barreled past our doorway, a percussive clanking sound of metal rolling over tracks hurtled past me.

Cable tracks carved into the ground, running down the middle of the street like the roots of an old oak tree, served as a signpost, pointing the way ahead. I begin to count the house numbers, each step bringing me closer to my childhood home.

As I stood at the street corner seeing the cable car tracks running all kinds of crazy in the middle of the intersection, electric excitement shot through me. Everything suddenly came alive in Kodachrome color. My breath quickened, and I felt the steadiness of the concrete under my feet. I was back.

"Ready?" Eric asked me.

"Yes. I'm ready," I replied, because my loving Jesus was crossing the street with me, just like He always had ever since I was born Bonnie Sook-Wah Lee in Chinatown many years ago.

Homecoming never felt closer.

* * *

Eric and I slowly walked up to find an old, fading, maize-yellow Victorian, its weathered wooden doorframe closed shut. There were paper signs taped all over the doors of the apartment and along the walls with blue tape. As we looked closer to read the notice, we discovered something unexpected.

The same weekend when I found this old childhood home was the very same weekend it was being demolished. Soon, something new would stand in its place, and I would never be able to see it again.

There were construction trucks parked on the street. So, I walked up the broken concrete steps and knocked on the door several times. Loudly.

Maybe the construction crew is still inside, preparing things before it gets torn down?

The door finally opened because, like a woodpecker, I did not stop knocking, and a tall man wearing a hard hat, gloves, and a tool belt looked down at me.

"You can't come in here!" he bellowed. "We're tearing this place down!"

"Oh no! Have you started yet?" I asked him a question to stall him while I figured out my appeal.

"Yes, right now. We are starting right now. This weekend!" he blared.

"Oh, my gosh! This is a miracle!" I told him.

Mr. Construction paused. I'd gotten his attention. This was my shot.

"This is the home I was born in! This is the first time I've been back in over 30 years! And it's the weekend it's going to be destroyed," I relayed.

"Oh, wow." Mr. Construction was intrigued. I got him.

Before he came to his senses, I pleaded my case. "I think it's meant to be, don't you think? If I came next weekend, it would've been gone. Can I please do one more walk-through?" I gave him my Bugs Bunny, pleading puppy dog eyes, hollering above all the racket of noise raining down all around us.

He hesitated, so I quickly added, "I promise I will be very careful. Just one walk-through. One minute. That's it, and I'll be out of here! Promise!" I placed my hands together like I was praying and said, "Pleeeeasse!"

"Okay. Just *one* walk-through. *One.*" Mr. Construction put up one finger. I nodded up and down. He smiled. "Go for it!"

I waved Eric over. "What? He's actually letting us in?" Eric's eyes were as big as saucers. "No way!"

"Yes way!" I exclaimed. And because we only got one walk-through, I asked Eric to record a video. I would talk about everything as we moved through the house.

We stepped through the door, crossed over the threshold, and began climbing the long flight of narrow wooden stairs.

This was exactly the way I remembered it.

At the top of the landing, the walls were already knocked down and gone, stripped bare, exposed beams all around us, and because the floors were in the middle of being demo'd out, I made my way carefully. I was amazed to find my feet knowing where to go because they still knew the layout of the house from memory.

There on my left stood the small kitchen and dining room, where I stood next to Ah-Ma as I watched her and my grandma Mah-Mah wash vegetables, chop, and cook, seeing tongues of fire flare under the wok as the women cooked.

Straight ahead of me, where the bay of windows let in the sunlight, was the living room, where my uncles watched television with the rabbit ears. We made our way down the hallway to the bedroom I shared with Ah-Ma and my father.

We stood in the bathroom where the clawfoot porcelain tub had once been, with the rubber plug on a chain that I played with when I was little. We poked our heads into three other bedrooms where Yeh-Yeh, my grandma, and the other family members lived.

As I did one final walk-through, I recognized I had everything I needed to build a new life with my children and my husband that is meaningful and beautiful, free with strength. What I needed to take with me on my journey to create a new future, I already possessed in my soul and in my stories.

Just because life feels broken doesn't mean it isn't beautiful.

Jesus whispers, *Brokenness is made beautiful because you are loved by Me.*

As Eric and I slowly descended the steep flight of stairs and closed the door behind us, I stepped off the broken concrete doorstep and onto the sidewalk. A sky of blue stretched above us. Sunlight touched my shoulder.

The scent of spring returning, like blossoms budding on the arms of a winter tree that once stood barren outside my window, imbued the air with sweetness. And all was right and beautiful in the world that day. Sweet like jasmine.

I finally belong. I have found my place in this world. I have found my true self.

I am God's beloved.

> I will heal their waywardness and love them freely...I will be like the dew to Israel; he will blossom like a lily (Hosea 14:4-5).

Parting Words

In the Chinese culture, the jasmine flower Mo Li Hua holds special meaning, inspiring a beautiful Chinese folk song dating back to the eighteenth century and still being sung today. The song "Mo Li Hua" poetically describes a custom of giving jasmine flowers as a gift. It is the most well-known Chinese song in the world, celebrated for its beautiful melody and lyrics.[1]

It is also one of the first songs I learned as a little girl, hearing its sweet melody in the streets of Chinatown.

I share it now with you.

Mo Li Hua // 茉莉花

What a beautiful jasmine flower
好一朵美麗的茉莉花

Budding and blooming here and there,
芬芳美麗滿枝椏

Pure and fragrant all do declare.
又香又白人人誇

Let me pick you with tender care,
讓我來將你摘下

Sweetness for all to share.
送給別人家

Jasmine flower, oh jasmine flower
茉莉花呀茉莉花

As a flower, jasmine is a sweet, aromatic, climbing flower, symbolizing elegance and grace.

Beloved friend, you are jasmine, bringing beauty and sweetness wherever you go. You are a beautiful gift of God, lovingly created to release the fragrance of Christ as you blossom and bloom. May you feel as beautiful and beloved as you truly are this very moment. Just as you are.

Sweet like jasmine.

NOTES

Chapter 1—Birth Certificate

1. "Understanding Chinese Characters," ChinaSage, accessed April 6, 2021, www.chinasage.info /chinese-characters.htm.

Chapter 2—The Silk Dress

1. "From Broken to Beautiful: The Power of Kintsugi," Concrete Unicorn, June 27, 2018, https:// concreteunicorn.com/blogs/journal/from-broken-to-beautiful-the-power-of-kintsugi.

Chapter 3—The Candy Store

1. Kay D. Weeks and Anne E. Grimmer, *The Secretary of the Interior's Standards for the Treatment of Historic Properties with Guidelines for Preserving, Rehabilitating, Restoring & Reconstructing Historic Buildings* (Washington, DC: U.S. Department of the Interior, National Park Service Technical Preservation Services, 2017), https://www.nps.gov/tps/standards/treatment-guidelines -2017.pdf, 77.

Chapter 4—Strange Medicine

1. Elizabeth Palermo, "Who Invented the Printing Press?" LiveScience, February 25, 2014, www .livescience.com/43639-who-invented-the-printing-press.html.

Chapter 5—Bookstore

1. Colin Chinnery, "Bookbinding," International DunHuang Project, accessed April 6, 2021, http:// idp.bl.uk/education/bookbinding/bookbinding.a4d.

Chapter 6—Noodle Shop

1. Choo Yilin, "5 Things You Didn't Know About Jade," January 5, 2018, https://blog.chooyilin .com/blog/5-things-you-didnt-know-about-jade.

Chapter 7—Vegetable Stand

1. To give context to the scope of 20 million lives lost, according to the National World War II Museum, the total American civilian and military deaths was 418,000.

2. "Rice Grain Porcelain," Gotheborg.com, accessed April 6, 2021, http://gotheborg.com/glossary /ricegrain.shtml.

Chapter 8—Women in the Mirror

1. C.S. Lewis, *The Four Loves* (New York: Harcourt Brace & Company, 1988), 71.

2. "Tradition of China—Hair Ornament Culture," ChinaFetching, accessed April 6, 2021, https:// www.chinafetching.com/tradition-of-china-hair-ornament.

Chapter 9—Fate

1. Emma Taggart, "Get a Handy Look at the History of Traditional Chinese Folding Fans," My Modern Met, June 20, 2020, https://mymodernmet.com/chinese-folding-fans-history.

Chapter 12—Homeland

1. "Chinese Architecture (si he yuan)," YouTube video, Chinese Learning Center of Miami, January 30, 2020, www.youtube.com/watch?v=FoaBbxJf9F0.

Chapter 13—Lotus Flower

1. Kelly Pang, "Chinese Lanterns: What They Are and How They're Used," China Highlights, March 18, 2021, www.chinahighlights.com/travelguide/culture/lanterns.htm.

Chapter 15—Limbo

1. "Christianity in China," https://en.wikipedia.org/wiki/Christianity_in_China.

Chapter 16—Red Bean Dessert

1. Joe DiStefano, "The Secrets of Cantonese Cooking, America's First Chinese Cuisine," Serious Eats, October 15, 2014, www.seriouseats.com/2014/10/introduction-what-is-cantonese-chinese-cuisine .html.

Chapter 17—Earthquake

1. Richard Gonzales, "Rebuilding Chinatown After the 1906 Quake," National Public Radio, April 12, 2006, www.npr.org/templates/story/story.php?storyId=5337215.

2. Leila de Vos Van Steenwijk, "Nature in Asian Art: A Guide to Symbols, Motifs, and Meanings," Christie's, April 19, 2016, www.christies.com/features/Nature-in-Asian-art-7220-1.aspx.

Chapter 21—Gift Basket

1. Abby Narishkin and Benji Jones, "Why a Bowl of Bird's Nest Soup Can Cost More than $100 at Some Restaurants," *Business Insider*, October 22, 2020, www.businessinsider.com/ birds-nest-soup-delicacy-asian-cuisine-culture-so-expensive-2019-2.

Chapter 23—Chinese Hospital

1. Guenter B. Risse, "Translating Western Modernity: The First Chinese Hospital in America," *Bulletin of the History of Medicine* 85, no. 3 (Fall 2011): 413-47, doi: 10.1353/bhm.2011.0066.

2. "Shang and Zhou Dynasties: The Bronze Age of China," The Metropolitan Museum of Art, October 2004, http://www.metmuseum.org/toah/hd/shzh/hd_shzh.htm.

Chapter 24—The Bakery

1. "History of Chinese Chops—Chinese Seals," Learn Chinese History, accessed April 6, 2021, www .learnchinesehistory.com/chinese-chops-seals-history.

Chapter 27—The Cup

1. Theodora Sutcliffe, "The Drink That Costs More Than Gold," BBC, April 26, 2016, www.bbc.com/ travel/story/20160425-the-pot-of-tea-that-costs-10000.

Parting Words

1. "Mo Li Hua," sin80, November 5, 2017, www.sin80.com/en/work/mo-li-hua.

Acknowledgments

The seed to write *Sweet Like Jasmine* was planted in my heart 11 years ago when readers started responding to a new series of blog posts I published about my journey to find my childhood home in San Francisco Chinatown. When I shared snippets of my story, readers became kindred spirits, sharing stories in return within the comments. I found kinship. But after a few entries, I stopped. I wasn't ready to tell my story.

But, through the loving, loyal online community of supporters and readers who helped launch my books *Finding Spiritual Whitespace* and *Whispers of Rest*, and the overwhelming number of heartfelt responses I received from women all over the world through the years, I gained the courage to write this book, knowing I wasn't alone. Kindred readers, thank you for your love. Thank you for recommending and gifting my books to friends and family. This book is here because of you.

Never in a thousand years could I have guessed that I'd be writing this book during a worldwide pandemic of the COVID-19 virus. It felt like an impossible task to write with the exhaustion and stress of being quarantined as our world spiraled into chaos, fear, and uncertainty. So, how was I able to write this book under unprecedented levels of stress? To accomplish this by faith, God brought in people to empower me to do the impossible.

Thank you, first, to Eric, my beloved soulmate and husband. Thank you for giving so much of yourself to get me across the finish line, giving me headspace to breathe and write by offering unwavering emotional support and practical help cooking dinners and doing grocery runs and soccer pick-ups and drop-offs. Day in day out, you heard me ping-pong between discouragement and inspiration. Thank you for praying for me and loving me so deeply. I love you forever.

Thank you to my beautiful children, Josh and Caleb, for encouraging me to tell my story and not worry about what others would think. Thank you for praying and being my first audience as I read chapters to you, always being very affirming. I'm so blessed to be your mom. I love you deeply.

Thank you to my incredible agent, Lisa Jackson, who fearlessly championed this book from the beginning, as one of the few Chinese American stories in the Christian space. Thank you for believing in my voice and in diversity, and for opening the way to get this book published. You guided me with the kind of business acumen, insight, and kindness that authors only dream of. I was able to write fearlessly because you made it easier to be brave.

Thank you to my publishing team at Harvest House. Working together to bring *Sweet Like Jasmine* to print was a joy. I'm grateful for the energy and expertise behind the marketing team led by Sherrie Slopianka and Jessica Ballestrazze, and for my publicists, Jana Muntsinger and Pamela McClure of MMPR, who gave reach and wings to this book. Special thanks to my amazing editor, Kathleen Kerr, the Michaelango of editing. Her skillful hands sculpted the manuscript, illuminated the storytelling, and amplified the heart of this book.

Thank you to the Patreon supporters who enable my online writing ministry, fueling me to write, podcast, and create content that encouraged tens of thousands of women. Special thanks to my generous ministry partners Lisa McGee and Mo-Yun Fong, who encouraged me deeply.

Thank you to my in-real-life friends who encouraged and prayed for me as I wrestled to write. I was able to be brave knowing I am loved and accepted by you. I'm so grateful for you: Carol Hursh, Sally Forster, Merrianne Young, Michelle Dunn, Hera Hong Lee, Elaine Wang, Katharina Krahn, Monica Paulin, Sofia Montejo, Amy Marsden, Henriette Vierra, Sandra Sharp, Juanita Li, Dr. John Patterson, and many more. Special thanks to Stephanie Bryant, Jennifer Dukes Lee, Jennifer Schmidt, and Becky Keife for being a light for me in this book's early days.

To the One who is my beginning, who will love me to the very end—*Jesus*. Thank You for never abandoning me, holding me close in Your never-ending, always-faithful love. I love You.

About the Author

Bonnie Lee Gray is the author of *Whispers of Rest* and *Finding Spiritual Whitespace*. An inspirational speaker and podcast host of *Breathe: The Stress-Less Podcast*, Bonnie touches thousands of lives every year using storytelling, soul care, nature, and prayer. Her writing is featured in numerous Christian media outlets, including *Relevant* magazine and *Christianity Today*. She lives in California with her husband and two sons. Connect with her at thebonniegray.com and on Instagram @thebonniegray.

Visit www.SweetLikeJasmine.com
to download free resources to spark conversation
and gather friends to host your book club.